The Connecting Church

BEYOND SMALL GROUPS TO AUTHENTIC COMMUNITY

RANDY FRAZEE

WILLOW CREEK
RESOURCES

ZONDERVAN™

GRAND RAPIDS, MICHIGAN 49530 USA

We want to hear from you. Please send your comments about this book to us in care of the address below. Thank you.

ZONDERVAN™

GRAND RAPIDS, MICHIGAN 49530 USA

WWW.ZONDERVAN.COM

ZONDERVAN™

The Connecting Church
Copyright © 2001 by the Willow Creek Association

Requests for information should be addressed to:

Zondervan, *Grand Rapids, Michigan 49530*

Library of Congress Cataloging-in-Publication Data
Frazee, Randy.
    The connecting church : beyond small groups to authentic community /
Randy Frazee.
      p.   cm.
    Includes bibliographical references.
    ISBN 0-310-23308-9 (hardcover)
    1. Community—Religious aspects—Christianity. 2. Community—Biblical
teaching. 3. Church. 4. Community life—United States. 5. Small groups—
Religious aspects. I. Title.
BV4517.5 .F73 2001
250—dc 21
                                                       00-051300
                                                           CIP

This edition printed on acid-free paper.

All Scripture quotations, unless otherwise indicated, are taken from the *Holy Bible: New International Version®*. NIV®. Copyright © 1973, 1978, 1984 by International Bible Society. Used by permission of Zondervan. All rights reserved.

Interior design by Todd Sprague

Printed in the United States of America

---

03 04 05 06 /❖ DC/ 10 9 8 7 6

In memory of my mother,
Ruth Ann Frazee

CONTENTS

ACKNOWLEDGMENTS

Writing a book on community is certainly not a solo sport. I have so many people to thank for making this work a reality. First and foremost, I thank Jesus Christ. I have never recovered from your gracious offer of life to me in 1974. Second, I want to dedicate this book in memory of my mother, who passed away in December of 1999. Her simple faith in God has spoken to the depths of my soul. I and my father Ralph, brother Don, and two sisters, Teresa and Jo Ann, miss her so much. She sacrificed her whole life for us so we could succeed. In this small way I want to publicly acknowledge my gratefulness for her life.

I want to thank my wife, Rozanne. I never dreamed when I met her at the age of fifteen that one person could so perfectly and courageously love a guy like me. Words cannot describe how deeply I feel about my wife, but I will spend the rest of my life trying. She also edited the manuscript before the editors at Zondervan got ahold of it. Her efforts have saved me a great deal of time and embarrassment, and once again she has made me look good. Our four children, Jennifer, David, Stephen, and Austin, truly inspire and motivate me. It was my vision for our life together that caused me to pursue these principles of community so passionately—not only to write about it but, more important, to live it.

To my fellow neighbors and followers of Jesus Christ, who have entered into the mystery and joys of Christian community, I want to thank you for seeing it and going for it. While I know the number of people with whom we share community will grow, I proudly list those who are here now—Gary, Linda, Lauren, and Steven Lawrence; Pat and Rita Ballow; Lisa, Jim, Brian, Kevin, Steven, and Scott Tally; Scott, Kendall, and Connor Huffman; Garrett and Preston Greer; Roger and Sue Wells; Rich, Susan, Rachel, and Christy Horton; Greg, Lynanna, Gregory, and Ryan Messer.

I want to thank the elders and people of Pantego Bible Church for being so passionate about the right things and so patient with me as we continue to define what it means to follow Christ in authentic community. Thank you for allowing me the time to share these concepts with the broader body of Christ. I truly love being your pastor. To my staff—*you're the greatest!* You believe the vision of community, you live it, and you are working with all your might to put it within reach of the people God has given us to shepherd. A crown awaits you in the kingdom to come.

I have the great fortune of having more people than I deserve come alongside and support me so unconditionally. You held me up when I was tired and discouraged, overlooked my quirks, and gave me more than one break. You saw more of God's vision in me than I could see myself— Bob and Linda Buford, George Gallup Jr., Dallas Willard, Larry Crabb, Gayle Carpenter, Bill Donahue, Howard Hendricks, John Castle, Lyle Schaller, Scott and Donita Jones, Mike Reilly, Rick Veigel, Larry Ivey, Don Guion, Jim

Hyde, Tom and Ruth Bulick, Pat and Rita Ballow, Darryl Taylor, Ed Frazier, Ryall and Jane Tune, Kevin Miller, Aubrey Malphurs. To those I have forgotten, once again I give you an opportunity to overlook my imperfections. I want to thank Rita Ballow for typing my manuscript and standing by me for ten years as my assistant. I want to thank Ruth Bulick for picking up the management of my life and ministry. I acknowledge that it may be one of the toughest jobs on the planet. If there is any good that I have done in my ministry, Rita and Ruth certainly share in the credit. Without them I could not have done half of what I have done. Thank you for your unconditional support. Viva la Rita and Ruth!

I want to thank Bill Hybels, Jim Mellado, Joe Sherman, Christine Anderson, Wendy Seidman, Nancy Raney, and the wonderful people of the Willow Creek Association for pursuing and believing in this project. A special thanks to Christine Anderson for spotting the idea for the book at a Willow Creek conference workshop I was teaching, and then sharing it with the people at Zondervan. Finally, I want to express my sincere thanks to the wonderful team at Zondervan—Jack Kuhatschek, Scott Bolinder, Jonathan Petersen, Alicia Mey, Stan Gundry, Dirk Buursma. You have given me a precious opportunity to put my passion for community into words. Thank you for being more than publishers and editors, which you do real well, but true partners. Jack, thanks for not only seeing the book but also the vision.

Randy Frazee, Arlington, Texas

FOREWORD

BY LARRY CRABB

Community matters. That's about like saying oxygen matters. As our lungs require air, so our souls require what only community provides. We were designed by our Trinitarian God (who is himself a group of three persons in profound relationship with each other) to live in relationship. Without it, we die. It's that simple. Without a community where we know, explore, discover, and touch one another, we experience isolation and despair that drive us in wrong directions, that corrupt our efforts to live meaningfully and to love well.

The future of the church depends on whether it develops true community. We can get by for a while on size, skilled communication, and programs to meet every need, but unless we sense that we belong to each other, with masks off, the vibrant church of today will become the powerless church of tomorrow. Stale, irrelevant, a place of pretense where sufferers suffer alone, where pressure generates conformity rather than the Spirit creating life—that's where the church is headed unless it focuses on community.

But focus is not enough. We need three additional elements: a well-developed theology of community, including an understanding of cultural factors that lead to its violation; a clear definition of community (insofar as something Spirit-created and fluid can be defined); and an intentional plan for churches to follow in moving toward community. The plan must include vision, goals, and strategies. And it must entice our hearts in the direction the Spirit is leading.

The Connecting Church, by my friend Randy Frazee, goes a long way in providing what we need. Randy is solidly rooted in biblical wisdom, he tackles head-on the cultural issues that stand in the way, he gives us a clear picture of what we're trying to develop, and he is practical without becoming formulaic.

More than anything else, though, two things stand out. First, a pastor's heart energizes the book. I think the Great Shepherd is well represented. Second, the daunting challenge the book lays out feels more enticing than intimidating. I came away from the book thinking, "My goodness, maybe churches really could become communities. All the talk about community might actually lead to action."

The Connecting Church is a powerful tool to help us see Christ's dream for his people come true.

FOREWORD

BY GEORGE GALLUP JR.

The small group movement in America, described by sociologist Robert Wuthnow as "a quiet revolution," is a hopeful one because it indicates that Americans, in our impersonal and fragmented society, see a vital need to reconnect with one another.

An estimated 40 percent of U.S. adults are involved in small groups of some sort that meet on a regular basis and include nurture and sharing. Six in ten of these groups are connected with a faith community.

If one assumes that the church's first priority is to develop disciples, then small groups must be regarded as an essential first step. Close inspection by Wuthnow and senior pastor Randy Frazee, however, reveals that such groups can become insular and self-serving, and do not necessarily lead people to "the rich, enduring fellowship we were created by God to experience," to use author Frazee's words.

Pastor Frazee does not want to "dismantle the small group movement in America," as he puts it, but to "take it to the next level." Toward this end, Frazee writes about factors that destroy the opportunity for more meaningful community, and he offers solutions. He also gives practical advice on how people can simplify their lives, setting the stage for deeper relationships with other people.

With encouragement and support from Bob Buford, and in consultation with his own staff and a board of advisers that included theologians, sociologists, survey researchers, educators, and others, Frazee developed the Christian Life Profile, a powerful discipling tool that he has already put to use in his own church, Pantego Bible Church, and with exciting results.

Building on the foundation of core beliefs, practices, and virtues of the persons being tested, the Profile helps people see the extent to which they are becoming "fully developing disciples"—that is, growing in both love for God and love for neighbor. This Profile is not only an excellent indicator of the level of spiritual maturity in a given congregation, it is also a powerful nurturing mechanism, helping people identify those areas that need further attention in order to grow spiritually.

With clear and forceful writing, Randy Frazee has produced a powerful book that answers key questions in the quest to become more like Jesus Christ: Where are small groups leading us? What steps should we take to build communities that exude "the presence, power, and purpose of Jesus Christ"? The Christian Life Profile, solidly grounded in experience and research, is an exciting and hopeful answer to the second question.

FOREWORD

BY DALLAS WILLARD

Randy Frazee's *The Connecting Church* begins from the lostness of our age, the profound loneliness and isolation that characterize contemporary American life "at its best." It addresses this condition from the point of view of the author's own experience, as well as from that of his role as a successful pastor of a thriving suburban church. It deals with this condition not only sociologically but also theologically, and especially with reference to the mission of Jesus in the real world of our present time. It does not offer an easy solution but confronts head-on the brutal individualism of current American life, which has also infected our religious institutions and rendered them largely ineffectual as avenues of redemption.

We no longer know in our society how to love our neighbors as ourselves—and rarely do we even see any attempt made. This is, unfortunately, also true of our "neighbors" with whom we go to church—who often live thirty miles away from where we live, and almost never live next door. (Thank God for any exceptions!)

All too often real-life connections simply run on a different track from "church" and remain unredeemed and unredemptive. The various churches are viewed as competing, voluntary associations appealing to the individualized needs of a passing public. And, sadly, even their small groups, or "cells," do not necessarily provide the community within which real neighbor-love is realized.

Randy Frazee gives concrete and well-researched plans, tested in his own church setting, for disrupting the public form of individualism that sin takes today in our "communities"—a form commonly mistaken for progress and prosperity. He shows a way that followers of Jesus can be together under God and in the practice of effectual neighbor-love, and how others can be brought to Jesus through the unmistakable manifestation of supernatural *agape* in their midst. His proposals will work on the small scale as well as on the large. They do not require large outlays of money, talent, or technique, and they can easily be adapted to local circumstances. Intelligently and prayerfully pursued, they will reliably serve to implement all aspects of Jesus' Great Commission wherever our congregations are located.

PREFACE: OPENING WORDS

I am the pastor of a very exciting church! In 1990, when I came aboard as Pantego Bible Church's senior minister, the church had been experiencing a severe decline, losing over two-thirds of its membership. Revitalizing this congregation took more than enthusiasm and willpower; it took a drastic re-visioning and the adopting of a new paradigm for ministry. To the congregation's credit, it weathered the transitions and changes, as well as the experimenting and trial and error that always accompany massive reengineering. In just ten years, the congregation had recovered, growing to five times the size it had been in 1990. It also orchestrated a relocation from its seven-acre site to a beautiful seventy-six-acre site on the main freeway that connects Dallas and Fort Worth. The outreach and growth potential is now unlimited.

One of the most significant things we did as a congregation was to add a churchwide small group ministry. It was not merely a nice add-on; rather, it was central to involvement in our church. We had many of our people involved in small groups. In our minds, we were experiencing the best of both worlds: We had quantitative growth (attendance) and qualitative growth (small group involvement).

Much to our surprise, one hot, sunny summer day we had a cooler of cold ice poured on us. I had taken my staff off-campus for a daylong meeting. We had a preestablished agenda—"small groups" was not on it. Before we began our opening session, somewhere in the room a conversation broke out. The topic was personal small group satisfaction. Someone on our staff had the audacity to confess that their small group experience was unsatisfying. Once the virus was airborne it spread like the black plague. One staff member after the other shared their disappointment. Now, if the corporate dissatisfaction had been aimed at proper lumbar support in our office chairs, that would have been one thing. However, we were confessing that our central vehicle for assimilation and spiritual growth wasn't working for the most motivated members of our church. I, too, shared my discontent.

The agenda quickly changed. We spent the entire day talking openly about the best-kept secret in our church: Small groups were not achieving authentic community. There is a Chinese proverb that says, "Whom the gods want to destroy they send forty years success." We had successfully rebuilt our church numerically, using the small group structure. Now we were faced with the awful reality that our system was not really working to accomplish the mission of discipleship in the lives of our people—including us who were leaders. While no structure is 100 percent successful, including the one we have now, I knew a change had to take place. However, our people were completely content with the progress the church had made. It became my job to convince people aboard the luxury liner *Titanic* that an iceberg was looming just ahead.

After eight hours of discussion we concluded that the problem was not with the *size* of the groups. The small group is an appropriate vessel for people to experience the necessary depth of intimacy required for transformation. However, merely being a small group was not enough. We discovered that the fault wasn't with the *people* who made up the small groups. They genuinely wanted to grow and to fulfill the mission Jesus had called them to fulfill. They were in the small groups we designed because we had told them it was the place they could achieve community.

What then is missing? became our central question. Thus began the journey to discover the characteristics that drive successful experiences of community, whether Christian or non-Christian. After studying effective places of community, such as the life Jesus had with the disciples, an Israeli kibbutz, a military base, L'Arche, and even the effective community of a gang, I identified fifteen characteristics of community, centered around common purpose, common place, and common possessions.[1] When I compared these to what is found in the typical American Christian small group movement, the gaps were glaring.

The purpose of this book is to bring this discovery to light and to share what we as a church have done and are doing with it. While the principles that undergird the characteristics are timeless and the concepts have been percolating in our congregation for years, we have been implementing the full ideas contained in this book only since the beginning of 1997. Admittedly, we are learning through trial and error, and what we are doing must be viewed as a process rather than as a completed program. It is my hope that as others read this book and venture out to implement these principles of community, they will share their stories with the larger body of Christ (see page 244 for a way to be part of the conversation). By doing so they will help us create a lifelong learning environment and make progress toward the rediscovery of authentic community.

While I will be presenting principles and applied methods, the search for authentic community is really more about experience and relationships. Therefore, I will unfold what I have to say about community through the lives of Bob and Karen Johnson. While the names are fictitious, every experience the Johnsons encounter is authentic to the real experiences in our town and church. Most of them I have experienced personally. You should identify easily with their story if you live in the suburbs, as two-thirds of Americans do. You will notice that the Johnson family has been created with a more favorable situation economically than many American families. I did this to dispel the notion that the solution to loneliness lies in just a little more money or a bigger house or a more expensive car.

My goal is not to dismantle the small group movement in America but to take it to the next level. You can have a small group and not experience community—but you cannot have community apart from a small group experience. This book is not so much a manual on small groups as it is a manual on the principles of biblical community. I would suggest that the most profound thought of the book is this: *Biblical community is the life of Christ on earth today.* When the church is fully functioning, it exudes the presence, power, and purpose of Jesus Christ. My prayer is that the words in this book and the experience of our particular church will contribute positively to an outbreak of authentic community in the Christian church.

1

THE LONELIEST NATION ON EARTH

To all appearances and by all standards the Johnsons have a wonderful life. They own a house in a nice suburb with four bedrooms, two baths, and a rear entry two-car garage. Their house is surrounded by a six-foot fence to provide privacy for an in-ground pool, barbecue grill, and patio furniture. Bob and Karen have two children—a boy and a girl. Each of them has a college degree; they both work and have a combined household income well above the average for their community. Most important, everyone in the family is in good health.

Yet if you could enter the hearts and thoughts of Bob and Karen Johnson, you would discover that they have dreams and fears no one else knows about. While they have never voiced it to anyone, there is an increasing sense of isolation, distress, and powerlessness growing inside of them. In a nutshell, the Johnsons have done a fine job "keeping up with the Joneses," but they still are not happy.

How could this be? The Johnsons are living the American Dream. There are so many people who are less fortunate. Actually, this personal dilemma, which is quietly gnawing away a sense of contentment in the Johnsons, is a national epidemic—and their experience is no surprise to sociologists and pollsters. George Gallup Jr. concluded from his studies and polls that Americans are among the loneliest people in the world.[1] This seems unbelievable when you think of the availability of transportation and the billions of dollars of discretionary money available for entertainment. Americans can buy so much activity—how can they possibly be so lonely? Today more than three-fourths of the American people live in metropolitan areas, and more than two-thirds of those live in suburbs.[2] We are surrounded by more people than ever before in the history of our country. With these undeniable benefits in place, how could a Gallup Poll rank us among the loneliest people in the world?

Let's take a closer look at the story of Bob and Karen. Eight years ago Bob took a job at an office located in a growing suburb. Although this took them further from their families, both Bob and Karen had agreed that it would still be feasible to fly home on occasion because they were making more money and the airport was in close proximity to their house. Bob and Karen both rise at 6:30 A.M. Bob rushes to leave the house at 7:00 to beat the rush hour traffic; doing so allows him to get to work in thirty-five minutes as opposed to fifty-five minutes. He opens the door leading into the garage, hits the garage door opener, gets into his car, and pulls out of the driveway. He spots his new neighbor taking out the trash and waves to him with a forced smile on his face. As Bob drives down the street, he reminds himself that his *new* neighbor has been in the neighborhood now for two years, and he still can't remember his name. This thought lasts for about five seconds before the radio is turned on, and Bob's mind now turns to the matters of the day.

Karen has worked out an arrangement to be at work at 9:00 A.M. so she can drop off her two children at school at 8:15. There is the usual rush to get herself and the two children ready and out the door by 7:55, but on this day she manages to pull it off. With the same ritual precision, Karen makes her way to the car and starts heading out the driveway when one of the children announces that he has left a lunch inside. The easiest move for Karen would be to go back in through the front door, but she sees her next-door neighbor, one of the few retired people in the area, beginning her yard work for the day. While Karen would love to catch up with her elderly neighbor, she is afraid if they engage in a conversation the children will be late for school—and then she'll be late for work. So rather than risk being late, Karen makes her way back to the rear entry garage, opens the door with the automatic opener, and goes inside. As she grabs the forgotten lunch from the kitchen table, she realizes she has forgotten to set the security system. Once this is accomplished, off she goes again.

Bob and Karen encounter an average day at work— nine-and-a-half hours at the office, completing only four-and-a-half hours of real productive work. Both will bring home bulging briefcases, in the hopes of sneaking in another hour of work after the children are in bed. At 3:30, the children go to their after-school program and wait for Mom or Dad to pick them up.

It is 5:00 P.M., and Bob absolutely must leave the office if he is to pick up the children on time from the after-school program. As it often goes, Bob doesn't leave until 5:20, and he gets trapped in a ten-minute traffic jam because of a stalled car on the freeway. He arrives at the school thirty minutes late. Everyone is just a little edgy.

Bob and the kids pull into the rear entry garage at 6:15. Bob turns off the security system, ensuring that no one has tampered with their home while they have been gone. Karen arrives at 6:30. The first order of business is dinner. Bob and Karen agreed two years ago, with a little help from a family therapist, that with Karen's return to work to help pay the bills, sharing household chores was going to be a vital part of suburban life; Bob would need to share the load with her in the evenings.

While the children watch television, Mom and Dad are working together to heat up a tray of frozen lasagna and garlic bread. After dinner, the dishes are cleaned up, the mail is perused, homework papers are checked, and the children get ready for bed. It is now 9:00 P.M. The children are a half hour late getting to bed, but it was the best they could do. At 9:15 Bob and Karen finally sit down. They are exhausted, really too tired to talk, so the television gets beamed on, right in the middle of some prime-time drama. They both watch television until the news is over, look at their briefcases for a moment, and agree to let the work go undone. Finally, at 11:30, they make it to bed. A couple of words are exchanged, mostly businesslike talk concerning tomorrow's details. As they close their eyes, they both ponder how easy this day was. The remainder of the weeknights will be filled with sports practices, games, music lessons, and some evening meetings at the office.

The next day the family rises again to engage in what has become a way of life for five out of the seven days of their week. But now, the weekend has arrived!

Saturday and Sunday are used for three primary activities: house and lawn care, children's sports, and church. These activities take up most of the available hours, but on the average weekend there are a few hours of open time to be used for soaking in life with family and friends. The problem the Johnsons have is common for many other contemporary couples. First, their extended family members live in other cities around the United States. Second, they were so busy during the week they didn't make plans to do something with another family. Finally, while they would be open to spending some spontaneous time with the neighbors, no one is out in their front yards except a few men mowing their lawns with earphones wrapped securely around both ears and the companion radio strapped to their khaki-colored shorts. Everyone else is either away from home or safely sheltered inside their centrally air conditioned/heated homes, fully equipped with cable television or satellite dish—or if not inside the house, they're in their backyards, which are completely landscaped for privacy.

Occasionally an outing is planned with another couple or family who may live in another part of town. The time always seems to be a positive experience—yet, because few of the gatherings are routinely with the same family, neither Bob nor Karen feels comfortable sharing their deepest dreams and fears. Another weekend comes to a close with unvoiced stress and boredom, and Bob and Karen individually conclude that this was an unusual week; next week will be better. Well, eight years have now passed since they adopted their "American Dream" lifestyle, with somewhere around 416 weeks classified as "unusual."

Oh, there is one more important aspect to the Johnsons' life. Bob and Karen are Christians. They attend church just about every Sunday and have been involved in a church-sponsored small group for a little over a year. The group is made up of other couples of roughly the same age and meets in one of the members' homes every other week.

The Sunday worship services are usually uplifting and inspiring. Bob and Karen feel a sense of satisfaction with their children's involvement in the Sunday school program. As a matter of fact, it was their desire to give their children a religious and spiritual foundation that brought them back to church after a lapse during college and their early years of marriage. While the church is extremely friendly, the only people they really know are those who attend their small group.

The Johnsons' small group usually meets on the first and third Thursday night of each month from 7:00 to 9:30. The members of the group rotate the task of hosting the meeting in their homes. Most of the members live about ten to twenty minutes away from each other.

Bob and Karen joined the group in the hopes of finding a surrogate extended family, or at least a set of close friends with whom they could share their dreams and fears. After a year's worth of faithful attendance to the group, the Johnsons started to miss some of the meetings. Why? There were several reasons. First, with their tight weekday schedule, it was diffi-cult to eat dinner, check homework papers, bathe the children, pick up a baby-sitter, drive to the small group get-together by 7:00, leave around 10:15, then take the baby-sitter back home, and return home around 11:30. This routine simply exhausted this couple, who were in search of meaningful friendships and a sense of personal peace.

A second reason the priority for the small group diminished was the children's sports games and practices. Both children play soccer and baseball—and one or both of the children have either a practice or a game on Thursday night.

A third reason was the disappointment the Johnsons were feeling over how seldom the members of the group got together outside of the regularly scheduled meetings. There seemed to be a mutual desire on everyone's part to get together, but something always seemed to prevent a more relaxed and spontaneous outing. Because the group only saw each other for a few hours twice (sometimes only once) a month, there wasn't the sense of intimacy the Johnsons wanted in order to feel free to really share their dreams and fears. While they would consider their small group members to be their closest friends, the Johnsons were longing for something more.

To look at the outside shell of the Johnsons' life, it would appear they have it all together, yet on the inside they are two of the statistically lonely people of whom George Gallup writes. Bob and Karen are just two of the millions of Americans who are searching to belong. Moreover, what is true of the Johnson family is intensified in the single-parent home. The activity for the adult parent is usually doubled, practically eliminating any time for the development of personal relationships. In addition, the single parent often has to burn a great deal of additional energy negotiating with the blended family members.

The single adult is not exempt from loneliness either. While more time can be allocated to enhancing adult relationships instead of managing children's activities, the additional time still leaves them at home many hours feeling deeply alone. While there is usually an active group of acquaintances, most singles still long for a deeper companionship than what seems to be in their grasp. One of the most significant struggles for a single person living in suburban America is the lack of wholesome gathering spots for singles. The lack of access to community means that isolation rules.

The purpose of this book is to help people who feel like the Johnsons find what they are searching for—to help people discover a rich sense of *community.* To belong! In our journey of discovery, we will explore three obstacles that hinder our attainment of biblical community in America. Three comprehensive and practical solutions will be offered to overcome these obstacles; these solutions will be more specifically defined in the fifteen characteristics that must be present in order for community to be experienced. The promise of this book is that restructuring our lifestyles around these fifteen characteristics will fulfill our "search to belong" and give us the rich, enduring fellowship we were created by God to experience.

2

CREATED FOR COMMUNITY

A few years ago my wife and I finally cracked under the pleas of our children to add a dog to the family. We gave in after eleven years of begging. Two days before Christmas, we purchased a full-bred beagle puppy we named Lady. She had lived with us for about a year when we took a family vacation without her. The children were very concerned about the well-being of Lady while we were away and insisted that if we couldn't take her with us that we get her the best possible accommodations. Through the help of another pet-obsessed friend, we located a place, The Pet Hotel—imagine that, a hotel for pets! This was the first I had ever heard of such a thing. Each pet is assigned an individual room. There is a television playing during the day for the dog to watch. The feedings are at precisely the time we offer them in her normal routine. The pets are actually walked and doted on more in The Pet Hotel than at home. This made the children feel better and made me feel a little poorer. (I have never been able to tell my father that I spent hard-earned money for an animal to stay in a pet hotel. For anyone born during the depression this would be an incomprehensible decision.)

The family returned home on a Friday night, too late to pick up Lady. So, the first order of business on Saturday was to head to The Pet Hotel. We gathered all her personal belongings, received a report ensuring us that they had done everything they promised, and paid the bill. When we got into the car, each of us eagerly petted Lady, genuinely happy to have her back. However, as we petted her, large clumps of hair clung to our hands. While I tried to convince the children that everything was okay, I was thoroughly concerned.

When we arrived home, I called the veterinarian in a panic. After I explained our dog's symptoms upon picking her up from our seven-day vacation, the doctor told me that Lady was stressed by our absence; he suggested we spend about two hours with her at home, and then her hair would stick once again. I seriously doubted the prescription, but the thought of avoiding a visit to the vet after paying the pet hotel bill worked for me. I kid you not, within fifteen minutes of being with us in our home, we couldn't pull a hair from Lady's body. It was quite unbelievable. The doctor was right after all.

If a dog starts to fall apart after just seven days of being robbed of community, how much more is it true for humans, who are created in the image of God for fellowship? We were designed by God physically, emotionally, and spiritually to require community for our health. In *The Gift of Touch,* Helen Colton says that the hemoglobin in the blood increases significantly when we are touched (hemo-globin is the part of the blood that carries vital supplies of oxygen to the heart and brain). She concludes that if we want to be healthy, we must touch one another.[1]

George Gallup Jr., referring to American isolationism, writes:

> We are physically detached from each other. We change places of residence frequently. One survey revealed that seven in ten do not know their neighbors. As many as one-third of Americans admit to frequent periods of loneliness, which is a key factor in the high suicide rate among the elderly.[2]

All this is said to drive home the point that community is not a luxury but a necessity for life.

A NEW OPERATING PRINCIPLE

The first thing Bob and Karen need to do is agree on an essential belief, or truth, about life that is almost as basic as breathing: People need to be involved in meaningful and constant community or they will continue on indefinitely in a state of intense loneliness.

One of the underlying problems of the Johnsons and most people who live in the average American suburb (or international equivalent) is that they have too many worlds to manage. There are too many sets of relationships that do not connect with each other but all require time to main-tain. Bob and Karen simply do not have enough time and energy to invest in each world of relationships in order to extract a sense of belonging and meaning for their lives.

Just think of the many disconnected worlds the Johnsons have to maintain: their own family, two places of work, church, a small group, the children's sports teams, the children's schools, extended family out of town, and neighbors. If we were to delve further into the Johnsons' lifestyle, we would discover many other worlds as well—old friends from high school and college, the last place they lived, and other relationship circles at church (for example, the women's Bible study group and the Mission Committee of which they are both members).

Prior to bringing a dog into our home, we tried to satisfy our children's longing for a pet by purchasing a hamster. The hamster seemed to spend most of its time spinning in a wheel in his cage. I recall how often I would look into the cage and say to myself, after experiencing a day filled with excessive activity but with an absence of real productivity and depth, "At least I got more done than you did!" The hamster's central problem is a lack of anything to do; our central problem is too much to do, too much to manage. Both scenarios produce the same result, namely, frustration. Many people today experience the same thing our hamster did—motion without meaning.

There is no quick and easy fix to solving the problem that the Johnsons, and millions of Americans as well, are experiencing. The solution does not lie simply in recommending a more meaningful activity while trying to preserve all the other worlds now in motion. If a true and workable solution is to emerge, it must involve a radical restructuring of our lifestyle. At the core of this restructuring is a new operating principle for living: *In order to extract a deeper sense of belonging, we must consolidate our worlds into one.* Just like someone who finds himself with too many creditors consolidates the many loans into one, so we must relieve ourselves of the stress of managing too many circles of relationships and move toward one main circle. The mission is to simplify our lifestyles in such a way that we concentrate more energy into a circle of relationships that produces a sense of genuine belonging. While this in no way suggests that we should be so narrow in our scope as to cut significant people out of our lives, it does reinforce the commonsense notion that we can go deeper with less to manage, and we *must* find a way to do this.

THE ROLE OF THE CHURCH

In this book I will suggest that the Johnsons and you look to the church to help you in your search to belong. In this postmodern age, the church is truly the one institution that has the function of community as part of its strategy to achieve its mission—which is the development of people who follow Jesus Christ. The author of Hebrews lays out the priority of community: "Let us not give up meeting together, as *some* are in the habit of doing, but let us encourage one another—and all the more as you see the Day approaching."[3]

The development of meaningful relationships where every member carries a significant sense of belonging is central to what it means to be the church. This is a God-ordained gathering of people that is so strong that even "the gates of Hades will not overcome it."[4] Yet, in the busyness of the American lifestyle, people who profess faith in

Jesus Christ and yet do not attend church make up the largest religious category in America. If the author of Hebrews were writing his words of challenge to us today, he would write, "Let us not give up meeting together, as *most* are in the habit of doing."

My purpose in this book is not to make anyone feel guilty for not managing the world of church, along with all the other worlds that demand his or her attention, but rather I want to provide you with a vision to make the church that inspires you central in your search to belong. The Bible clearly teaches that God intends to accomplish his primary purposes through the church. The first Christians understood that a decision to follow Christ also included a decision to make the church the hub of their world, even when it required the abandonment of existing social structures. Yale University professor Wayne Meeks makes this point, based on his meticulous research of the early church: "To be 'baptized into Jesus Christ' signaled for Pauline converts an extraordinary thoroughgoing resocialization, in which the sect was intended to become virtually the primary group for its members, supplanting all other loyalties."[5] The experience of authentic community is one of the purposes God intends to be fulfilled by the church.

Some of you may have tried church and have given up (if not literally, perhaps emotionally), because you were receiving a minimal return on your investment of precious time. Some of you stopped attending, not because you were against church but because you found its impact not significant enough to make the short list of activities for which you had time. I suspect you may be more ambivalent toward church than against it—a reasonable attitude if you see church as merely another world to manage. Yet, the writings of Scripture lead one to conclude that God intends the church, not to be one more bolt on the wheel of activity in our lives, but the very hub at the center of one's life and community. This is what God wants us to understand about the church of which he calls us to be a part.

If the church is going to accomplish this divinely inspired purpose in a postmodern world, it must do some restructuring. In a speech to a group of pastors, Lyle Schaller, a leading church consultant, has suggested what this restructuring might entail: "The biggest challenge for the church at the opening of the twenty-first century is to develop a solution to the discontinuity and fragmentation of the American lifestyle."[6]

The church of the twenty-first century must do more than add worlds to an already overbooked society; it must design new structures that help people simplify their lives and develop more meaning, depth, purpose, and community. While it is most desirable for the entire church to be focused on this restructuring, in reality, the solution can begin to take root with a small group of Christians from any local church. These Christians must be focused on experiencing what God intended and created us to have— biblical community as members of the body of Christ. However, there are some major, and often ignored, obstacles in the way that must be faced head-on if we ever hope to connect to authentic community. The next chapter will introduce you to the first of three barriers to community.

PART 1

CONNECTING TO A COMMON PURPOSE

3

THE PROBLEM OF INDIVIDUALISM

The 1998 Dreamworks hit movie *Antz* opens with worker ant Z sitting in an ant psychiatrist's office, relating his woes of living in a modern urban ant colony. It is a parody of contemporary urban life. Z says (in the voice of Woody Allen):

> All my life I have lived and worked in the big city, which, now that I think of it, is a problem. Since I always feel uncomfortable around crowds—I mean I have this fear of enclosed space. Everything makes me feel trapped all the time. I always tell myself that there has to be something better out there, but maybe I think too much. I think everything must go back to the thought that I had a very anxious childhood, you know; my mother never had time for me. You know, when you're the middle child of five million you don't get any attention. I mean how is it possible? And I have always had this abandonment issue, which plagues me. My father was basically a drone, like I've said. And, you know, he flew away when I was just a larva. And my job—don't even

get me started on it because it really annoys me. I was not cut out to be a worker—I'll tell you that right now. I feel physically inadequate. My whole life I have never been able to lift more than ten times my own body weight. And when you get down to it, handling dirt, you know, is not my idea of a rewarding career. It is the whole gung-ho super organization I can't get—I have tried but I can't get it. What is it? I am supposed to be doing everything for the colony. And what about *my* needs? What about me? I gotta believe there is someplace out there that's better than this. Otherwise I will just curl up in a larva position and weep. The whole system makes me feel insignificant.[1]

Some of the same angst articulated by Z is what many urban and suburban people feel today. We want to be noticed and feel special. We want to be individuals, not just some cog in the wheel. *"What about* my *needs?"* becomes our most important question.

The mores of this urban ant exemplify a major shift in our society, called *individualism* or the *"me culture"* by many culture specialists. This focus on the individual goes way beyond the issue of human dignity, the rights of the individual, or even the celebration of human uniqueness and diversity. All these things are maintained in healthy places of community. Individualism is a way of life that makes the individual supreme or sovereign over everything. Consider the list of characteristics of individualism over against its counterpart:

- Think of Myself over Think of Others *(If I don't, who will?)*

- Lawsuits over Reconciliation
- Individual Rights over Community Responsibilities
- Career Advancement over Company Loyalty
- Cynicism over Trust *(If you don't know anybody, how can you trust them?)*
- Relative Truth over Absolute Truth (truth is defined by and for each individual)

At the end of *Antz,* Z ultimately find himself sacrificing for and serving the community to which he belonged. The individual is valued in community, but ultimately the community collectively values something larger than themselves as individuals. This is the lesson Z learned. For the Christian community, Christ is valued over all others.[2] The Christian faith boldly and counterculturally invites us to think of others as more important than ourselves.[3]

One of Bob and Karen Johnson's key obstacles in this search to belong is something they very likely haven't thought about much. The Johnsons were not born into a culture of community but into a culture of individualism. In the simplest of terms, this means that when we gather in a room, we gather as a group of individuals who are concerned about our individual wants and needs, not as a community united around some common characteristics.

Most Americans see individualism as positive, as something that promotes free will, free markets, good self-esteem, free choices. However, after fifty years of unrestricted individualism, we have come face-to-face with its dark side, particularly as it relates to our search for community.[4] John Locke, chairman of the Department of

Human Communication Sciences at the University of Sheffield in England, has written about our contemporary social dysfunction in his book *The De-Voicing of Society: Why We Don't Talk to Each Other Anymore*. He labels this Western condition as *atomization*—people drifting away from each other. He suggests, like many culture experts, that the virtue of individualism grew in America after World War II.[5] Writing in the mid-nineteenth century, Alexis de Tocqueville observed that prior societies did not even have a word for *individualism,* which we have coined for our own use, because in their time there was indeed no individual who did not belong to a group and who could be considered as absolutely alone.[6] We have become, in the words of Locke, *solo sapiens.*

It seems undeniable that individualism erodes a sense of community. Education and culture expert E. D. Hirsch, the author of a wonderful book titled *Cultural Literacy,* helps provide a solution. At the end of his book, Hirsch provides a list of key people, events, and literature that have helped to define America's vision, values, and purpose. He suggests that the American people should be literate about and share a common understanding of these matters. For example, Abraham Lincoln's name is contained in the list of key people. When Lincoln's name is mentioned, there should be shared knowledge among Americans that he was the sixteenth president of the United States. In addition to this factual piece of information, an emotional response should arise concerning an important document signed by Lincoln—the Emancipation Proclamation. A bedrock value of the American society is the belief expressed in this proclamation, namely, that "all people are created equal."

Hirsch strongly suggests that if we cease to share our history and a common belief as a people, we will cease to be Americans.[7] There is a huge difference between being an American and being a group of people who happen to reside on American soil.

This mode of individualism is in full force today under the guise of American society. It isn't something the Johnsons chose; it is something into which they were born. Anyone born after World War II will feel the impact of individualism every day. Because the Johnsons were born into it, they really have no concept of an alternative society—one based on community and rooted in common values and purposes. Because they've never experienced the alternative, they have a hard time seeing the problem with individualism.

This breakdown of common beliefs and purposes has not only plagued American society but the American church as well. The "hard to swallow" premise is that today's church is not a community but rather a collection of individuals. The purpose of this statement is not to place blame on church leaders or parishioners but merely to be descriptive of the way things are. As a matter of fact, this pervasive attitude of individualism has greatly frustrated most church leaders. It has caused many a pastor or priest, whether privately or publicly, to scold their people for a lack of commitment to the church. Only now are we beginning to understand just how unrealistic this call to commitment is, given the lifestyle advocated by an individualistic culture.

If the truth be told, most people long to make a commitment to a community—because that is the way God designed us. The only adjustment to the original design of creation was the addition of human community—man was not made to be alone.[8]

Deep down, people want community but don't know how to get to it. If church leaders take an honest and hard look, we might discover that we haven't really been offering a solution that encourages community. Take small groups, for instance. Bob and Karen joined a church-sponsored small group in hopes of getting connected to community, but it didn't work. Why not?

The reflections of John Locke are instructive here. Throughout his book, *The De-Voicing of Society*, Locke traces the journey to our current "autistic society." In chapter after chapter he unpacks the choices we have made, as well as the subsequent consequences of de-voicing a society. It is an insightful analysis, but rather depressing. In the book's final chapter ("Vocal Warming"), it appears as though Locke is going to present practical solutions to this epidemic of individualism. Instead, this chapter dismantles and debunks each contemporary solution, including small groups, as falling short of a decisive victory. He writes:

> If small groups are thought of as a solution to desocialization, I'm afraid the news isn't very good. Few think they work, at least on a personal level. . . . Princeton's Robert Wuthnow has found that small groups mainly "provide occasions for individuals to focus on themselves in the presence of others. The social contract binding members together asserts only the

weakest of obligations. Come if you have time. Talk if you feel like it. Respect everyone's opinion. Never criticize. Leave quietly if you become dissatisfied."

In *Overcoming Loneliness in Everyday Life,* two Boston psychiatrists, Jacqueline Olds and Richard Schwartz, suggest that because of their episodic nature, groups "fail to replicate the sense of belonging we have lost. Attending weekly meetings, dropping in and out as one pleases, shopping around for a more satisfactory or appealing group—all of these factors work against the growth of true community."[9]

We have brought our mind-set of individualism into our small groups and therefore made them dysfunctional as effective places of true community.

Wuthnow probes this dysfunction further in *Sharing the Journey: Support Groups and America's New Quest for Community.*[10] He methodically presents his research of the small group movement in America in the last twenty-five years and suggests that this movement has emerged because church leaders are seeking to provide a solution to people's longing for belonging. The overwhelming conclusion of Wuthnow's research is that the small group is an improvement over the status quo—multiple church services where people sit in rows and look at the backs of other people's heads.

However, a major problem exists in the average small group experience. Wuthnow brings to the surface the fact that most small group members do not enter the group with a common set of beliefs and purposes. Rather, everyone carries his or her own individual set of beliefs and purposes.

Now, the most common response to this statement is to celebrate the value of each individual's right to hold whatever views they deem right and best for them. Given the number of strong leaders who have inflicted abuse—even spiritual abuse—on others through coercing and shaming people into "destructive" group thinking, this would not be a completely invalid position to take. However, when one holds this line of thought in the context of being isolated by individualism, it tends to produce in the church an operating value that the church has criticized secular society for adopting, namely, "unrestricted tolerance."

If a group of people does not share any common beliefs and purposes, then the highest virtue must be to tolerate each person's beliefs and behavior. Certainly there is a great need for tolerance in matters of personal style—that is, our preferences in how to raise children wisely, how to spend money responsibly, and what route to take to get to a restaurant. But is there a person who would go on record to say that a society can stand indefinitely without shared convictions on bedrock matters such as human life, human dignity, and environmental or creation management? Whoever is willing to embrace this notion hasn't looked historically at the collapse of societies such as that of the Roman Empire, which failed to advance these bedrock truths.

The average American Christian would undoubtedly embrace the words above as a valid indictment of the state of the American society. It is, however, more difficult to see that contemporary Christians are guilty of the same thing. Is the church currently mirroring the culture? If so, how can this be? Let's go back to Robert Wuthnow's research. He observed that when the average small group member shares a particular struggle in his or her life, along with the decision on how to handle the struggle, other group members are not in a position to challenge what is shared—even if they sense that the decision being made might harm the other person. The most common response is to say nothing; the most aggressive response is to timidly suggest that this isn't the course of action they would personally take. Now, if the decision involves the breed of cat to purchase or the menu selection for an upcoming wedding anniversary, then a nonchallenging response is appropriate. But what if the decision is to leave one's spouse, or to buy something that will put a person in massive debt, or to embrace the view that all religions lead to the same God? Or more realistically, what if the issues center around how to resolve a strained relationship or whether to make a career change? Applying Scripture to such practical issues is central to living as a follower of Jesus Christ.

In our contemporary secular culture, a codependent person is defined as one who enables a person to continue in his or her destructive behavior, such as alcohol or substance abuse. The difference between a codependent person and a tolerant person is determined by the nature of the behavior of the other person: If the behavior is seen as moral and nondestructive to herself and others, then the confronting person is considered tolerant; if the behavior is immoral and destructive to herself and others, then the confronting person is considered codependent.

Consider this foundational question: Does the Christian faith offer a basic set of beliefs, values, practices, and virtues that can be classified as absolutely true and totally essential for a constructive and fruitful life? If one holds a high view of the validity of the Bible as God's revealed word and his will, then the answer would most definitely be yes. Look closely at the rich and inspired writings of the apostle Peter:

> *His [God's] divine power has given us everything we need for life and godliness through our knowledge of him who called us by his own glory and goodness. Through these he has given us his very great and precious promises, so that through them you may participate in the divine nature and escape the corruption in the world caused by evil desires.*
>
> *For this very reason, make every effort to add to your faith goodness; and to goodness, knowledge; and to knowledge, self-control; and to self-control, perseverance; and to perseverance, godliness; and to godliness, brotherly kindness; and to brotherly kindness, love. For if you possess these qualities in increasing measure, they will keep you from being ineffective and unproductive in your knowledge of our Lord Jesus Christ. But if anyone does not have them, he is nearsighted and blind, and has forgotten that he has been cleansed from his past sins.*
>
> *Therefore, my brothers, be all the more eager to make your calling and election sure. For if you do these things, you will never fall, and you will receive a rich welcome into the eternal kingdom of our Lord and Savior Jesus Christ.*[11]

There is a basic and essential set of beliefs, values, practices, and virtues set out in the Bible, while still leaving room for disagreement on the nonbasic and nonessential issues. Robert Wuthnow suggests that one of the major problems with the small group in America is that people do not enter these groups with a common understanding and commitment to these *basic* tenets of the Christian faith. They may acknowledge that their church has a doctrinal statement of beliefs, but often they do not understand the relationship of these beliefs to daily life and therefore are not really committed to them for everyday living. Therefore, these beliefs have no real practical presence or influence in the small group. Everyone has their own individual idea, or absence of an idea, as to what the Christian life is all about; consequently, it becomes difficult for the individual to achieve that which he or she either doesn't personally know about or doesn't share in common with the other members of the team.

This is an important point to emphasize, because many people assume that the *churched* Christian has a firm handle on the biblical theology that fuels the Christian life. An extensive Barna Research Group study shows that "Americans' Bible knowledge is in the ballpark, but often off base."[12] More specifically, the survey found that Americans have strongly held theological positions, but that these positions often conflict with biblical views. The greatest challenge to churches may be dealing with the fact that most adults *think* they have both extensive and accurate Bible knowledge. Among the significant findings of the research are the following:

- On eleven of the fourteen belief statements tested, a majority of adults hold a view that is generally consistent with the Bible.

- When researchers examined the beliefs that people held strongly, in only two out of fourteen cases did a majority have both a biblically consistent view and hold it firmly.
- Few adults lack feelings about core biblical teachings; there was not a single item among the fourteen tested for which ten percent or more said they did not have an opinion about the statement.
- The statements for which the largest percentage of adults hold an opinion in conflict with Scripture were that "the Bible teaches God helps those who help themselves" and that "the Holy Spirit is not a living entity but is a symbol of God's presence or power."

Let's go back to the insights of E. D. Hirsch, tweak them a bit, and apply them to the church: "Can a group of Christians who do not share a common set of beliefs, practices, and virtues really be considered a Christian community, or are they rather a group of individuals who happen to gather on Christian soil?" This is something to ponder. We're not talking about people who do not attend church; we're not talking about people who do not embrace Christ as the Savior and Son of God. We are talking about people who simply don't know how the Christian life works. It is not that Christians do not want to or wouldn't embrace a clear, biblical definition of faith if given the opportunity.

Dallas Willard, professor at the University of Southern California's School of Philosophy, offers this observation: "By the middle of this [twentieth] century, [the church] had lost any recognized, reasonable, theologically and psychologically sound approach to spiritual growth, to really becoming like Christ."[13] Willard goes on to offer this indictment against the church for its failure to offer a substantive understanding of the Christian life: "What we are dealing with here is what created Western Civilization as a civilization. If all you had was what churches give out today, you would never produce Western Civilization."[14] Now, one of the chief ingredients of individualism's value system is to reject the notion of sharing something, particularly beliefs, in common with others. This rejection presents the greatest obstacle in overcoming the plague of individualism. The current view of many in our culture is that seeking communal adherence leads to abuse of power or to lording someone's beliefs and practices over community members. There are many experiences to lay on the table to validate this charge. However, the solution cannot be to abandon the principles of community for the principles of individualism; the solution is to provide boundaries and promote healthy principles of community.

I would suggest that we should thoughtfully challenge this contemporary view of communal adherence. John introduced the coming of Jesus with these words: "For the law was given through Moses; grace and truth came through Jesus Christ."[15] In the most basic sense, Jesus always deals with us in truth but does so in a gracious way. For example, Jesus told us that we were sinners—those who offended God (the law shows us this as well). The reason he told us this is because it's true. Now, this may be, and certainly was in Jesus' day, offensive to some. However, in Jesus' relationship with others, he never dealt with them in any other manner than a truthful one. It is absolutely true that all people "have sinned and fall short of the glory of God."[16] When Jesus met the woman at the well in Samaria, he confronted her with the truth of her failed marriages and current "live-in" situation.[17] When he dealt with the woman caught in adultery who was about to be stoned by a group of hypocritical men, he identified her actions as sinful.[18]

However, in contrast to the religious leaders of his day, Jesus always dealt with people in a grace-filled way. For all sinners, he graciously died on the cross to pay the debt we owed for our sins. For the Samaritan woman at the well, he offered "living water" as a real solution to her broken life. For the woman caught in adultery he rescued her from a lynch mob by creatively chasing them away.

For Jesus, to be gracious without speaking the truth would ultimately be destructive and harmful to the person. To be truthful without being gracious would simply be "inhuman" behavior. The alternative to the contemporary tolerance that asks us to lay aside basic truths in our relationships with others is to do what Jesus did—to deal with others in "grace and truth." As Christians the practical application to our life in community is to always uphold the basic elements of the Christian faith as revealed in the Bible but to dispense this truth in a gracious way.

To do what Jesus did should go a long way toward preventing spiritual abuse and legalism. The apostle Paul confirmed the teaching and practice of Jesus by saying that we should speak the truth "in love."[19] Whenever this takes place in Christian community, "the whole body, joined and held together by every supporting ligament, grows and builds itself up in love, as each part does its work."[20]

While this may not be the experience of the majority of Christian churches or small groups at present, it can be achieved. The prevailing mind-set of individualism is a serious obstacle to community—it was for the Johnsons, and it may well be for you, too! But it doesn't have to be.

4

FINDING A COMMON PURPOSE

The church has become a collection of individuals, due at least in part to the prevailing mind-set of individualism in our culture. This is the conclusion I reached in chapter 3. In this chapter I want to offer what I see as the principal solution to overcoming the devastating effects of individualism on our search to belong. The answer is simple and straightforward: We must have a common purpose. We must once again come together around shared beliefs and values. Bob and Karen must become a part of such a community, or their search will continue indefinitely.

Historian Wayne Meeks makes the following comment, based on his extensive research of the social world of the first-century church: "One peculiar thing about early Christianity was the way in which the intimate, close-knit life of the local groups was seen to be simultaneously part of a much larger, indeed ultimately worldwide, movement or entity."[1] Psycholinguist John Locke would agree. After classifying contemporary society as the first society with attention deficit disorder, Locke writes, "From a physical standpoint, a community is a collection of individuals, but the residents of a true community act like members of something that is larger than themselves."[2]

FIVE CHARACTERISTICS OF COMMUNITY AROUND A COMMON PURPOSE

The principle of sharing a common purpose is not new; it is an ancient principle that must be rediscovered. Its presence is simply not optional if you want true community.

If you were to study places where community exists, you would find the embodiment of the characteristics that uphold a common purpose. What are these characteristics?

Authority

In a community united around a common purpose there is a clear understanding of and respect for the *authority structure*. Someone is responsible to lead the community in such a way that it upholds and advances the common purpose. It is this authority structure that blesses and reinforces positive behavior, and holds community members accountable for negative or destructive behavior. In the typical American Christian small group, we love to use the word *accountability*. But if we are precise in our definitions, we really don't have accountability; we only have *disclosure*. A group member is often willing to disclose personal struggles and decisions, but there usually is no invitation to challenge the choices or to hold the person accountable to an objective standard.

True accountability calls for the appropriate and wise use of authority and leverage. If a group today seeks to exercise authority over a member who is pursuing an unacceptable standard (for example, an unbiblical divorce or a marriage to a non-Christian), this member will very likely simply leave the group. Because most people don't want him or her to leave, the member's actions and attitudes are never challenged. Often, the destructive actions or the disintegration of a relationship are not known by the other members until it's too late to step in and lovingly address the situation.

In the Old Testament nomadic community of Abraham, it was clear that Abraham was the authority, the patriarch. In the first-century church of Jerusalem, the authority was Peter. In the first-century culture, the head of the household was responsible for the nuclear family (the *oikos*), and all aspects of society supported this structure. Wayne Meeks writes:

> The head of the household, by normal expectations of the society, would exercise some authority over the group and would have some legal responsibility for it. The structure of the *oikos* was hierarchical, and contemporary political and moral thought regarded the structure of superior and inferior roles as basic to the well-being of the whole society.[3]

In the Amish community, there is a head elder, who is respected and who has authority to watch over and administer the values and beliefs of the community. In the tight-knit community of a monastery, the abbot (meaning "father") guides the monks toward their ultimate purpose of achieving union with God. Even gangs, which have emerged in large part because of a lack of healthy public places where community can be experienced, have a clearly established leader. Their purpose may be a destructive purpose, but the purpose is clear and the authority is in place.

The average reader may be thinking, *This kind of authority structure and accountability will never work in America.* If this is true, it is because a culture of individualism won't let it happen. As a matter of fact, all characteristics of community are countercultural! Open disclosure is a fine value to have in a group, but it won't produce genuine community. The characteristic of authority *must* be present. Yes, there are abuses that must be guarded against, but abandoning authority is not a workable solution.

Common Creed

Another characteristic of effective communities of purpose is a *common creed*—a shared understanding of the beliefs and practices that guide the community. For a twelve-step group, it is the twelve steps themselves; for the children of Israel, it was the Law.

Throughout the centuries, the Christian church has felt the need to establish common creeds. For the first-century urban church, Wayne Meeks observes that it was not just "shared content of beliefs but also shared forms by which the beliefs are expressed [that] are important in promoting cohesiveness. Every close-knit group develops its own argot [private vocabulary], and the use of that argot in speech among members knits them more closely still."[4]

Martin Luther, one of the great Protestant Reformers, felt compelled to create a common creed in the 1500s. The Augsburg Confession, written by Luther's friend and colleague Philipp Melanchthon, laid out the twenty-one articles of faith that guide the beliefs and practices of the

Lutheran Church. After visiting some of the churches and realizing that the Confession had not made its way to the pew, Luther wrote a "smaller" catechism comprised of questions and answers pertaining to the Ten Commandments, the Apostles' Creed, and the Lord's Prayer.

John Calvin, another great Reformation leader, developed the Geneva Catechism for the Reformed Church in 1536. The Religious Society of Friends (Quakers) developed a creed in the 1600s. The Roman Catholic Church published a creed from the Council of Trent in 1566, known as the Roman Catechism. In 1885 a new creed for Catholics was published in America, called the Baltimore Catechism. The Church of England has the Book of Common Prayer, divided into two parts—the first explains the baptismal covenant, the Apostles' Creed, the Ten Commandments, and the Lord's Prayer, while the second explains the sacraments of baptism and the Eucharist. In 1645 the Presbyterians developed the Westminster Confession of Faith.

In the last fifty years, the existence, or certainly the vitality, of a common creed is almost nonexistent in the American church. The declining mainline denominational churches appear to have inherited one or more, as is evident from the above paragraphs, but it does not appear to be meaningful to the majority of members. For the most part, the fast-growing contemporary church does not have a common creed or confession. The litmus test is to walk into any church and randomly ask the members to articulate the common creed that binds them together. A blank stare will be the overwhelming response. A culture of individualism does not like a common belief system; it even pawns it off as dangerous. However, every effective place of community has a common creed.

Traditions

A true community uses *traditions* to perpetuate the purpose and common creed and pass them on to the people of that community, particularly to the children. Traditions are things you do in the same manner, at the same time, which hold great value in communicating meaning to the people of the community. A tradition can be a symbol or festival or any activity that reinforces the beliefs, values, practices, virtues, and purposes of a community.

On a military base, for example, a long and carefully perfected list of traditions has been put in place to remember something significant, to communicate an important military value, or to honor a soldier who exemplifies the military values. Awards ceremonies for heroism are chock-full with rich tradition. A particular badge, medal, or stripe is used for particular deeds and given out by a particular person in authority in a very particular way. The military funeral is another event defined by tradition. The presentation to the spouse of the neatly triangular-folded American flag and the twenty-one-gun salute are just two traditions used to communicate honor, community, and meaning.

The people of Israel have built-in traditions, such as the Passover, the Feast of Booths, Hanukkah, the Year of Jubilee, and the like to recount God's faithfulness and to instruct the community in the principles of the Law. Tradition was the central means of passing on the faith to the next generation. Consider these words recorded by Moses:

In the future, when your son asks you, "What is the meaning of the stipulations, decrees and laws the LORD our God has commanded you?" tell him: "We were slaves of Pharaoh in Egypt, but the LORD brought us out of Egypt with a mighty hand. Before our eyes the LORD sent miraculous signs and wonders—great and terrible—upon Egypt and Pharaoh and his whole household. But he brought us out from there to bring us in and give us the land that he promised on oath to our forefathers. The LORD commanded us to obey all these decrees and to fear the LORD our God, so that we might always prosper and be kept alive, as is the case today. And if we are careful to obey all this law before the LORD our God, as he has commanded us, that will be our righteousness."[5]

For the first-century church, Jesus established Communion, or the Eucharist, to remember his death until he comes again.[6] And as one reads the book of Acts, it's clear how important baptism was to the early church.

Just as a culture of individualism scorns a common creed, so too it disdains tradition. While some traditions clearly need to be reevaluated, and done away with on occasion, all places of true community have them as an important part of their life together. If we are to rediscover community, we must revitalize old, or create new, traditions that impart our purposes, values, and beliefs into our thinking.

Standards

Another characteristic found in places of community is the presence of *standards*—a list of written or unwritten guidelines that define what is expected of the people of the community. These standards lay out what is considered normal behavior. For example, in the traditional Amish community, marriage to an outsider is condemned. Members of the community are expected to wear plain clothing with hooks and eyes as fasteners instead of buttons. If you had lived in a Benedictine monastery at any time in the last fourteen hundred years, you would be very familiar with the seventy-three chapters of the *Rule of St. Benedict,* which lay out the standards for living in the monastery. The rule book details everything from showing reverence at prayer to describing how monks are to sleep.

Today's culture has a hunger for spirituality and a true sense of community; many people are looking intently at the mystical relationship with God as it is carried on within the walls of the monastery. What the individualistic American in search of a spiritual experience must understand is that a long list of standards for proper conduct are part of the package deal, along with the candles, the incense, and the mystical encounters with Christ in community.

While this characteristic of community is found in centuries of communal life from the beginning of time until the present and is an essential component of healthy and effective community, here too our culture of individualism resists common standards.

We want community—but few seem open to the characteristics that promote it and sustain its life. If we want community, we must factor in this countercultural practice of following standards.

Common Mission

Any true community will have a clearly defined mission that brings the individuals of a group together and knits them into a cohesive family. For the military platoon sharing a foxhole, the mission could be to secure a town, blow out a bridge, take a hill, or protect a dignitary; for the Amish community, it is the preservation of a way of life and separation from the negative effects of modern-day culture; for the recovery group, it is freedom from addiction. (So powerful is the sense of common mission in drawing people together that M. Scott Peck calls the recovery group one of the most effective places of community today.) When you come across a place of community that truly works, you will discover that they share a common mission that is larger than any one person.

THE COMMON PURPOSE OF CHRISTIAN COMMUNITY

Having a common purpose is precisely what made the first-century church in Jerusalem so dynamic. Luke records these words in the book of Acts: "All the believers were together, but they all had their own ideas as to why they were there." Wait a minute—that's not what it says! The verse reads: "All the believers were together and had everything in common."[7] Do you wonder what that means? Just two verses earlier Luke says that the believers "devoted themselves to the apostles' teaching and to the fellowship, to the breaking of bread and to prayer"[8]—to a distinct set of beliefs and practices. They did this together. They were all on the same page; they had a common purpose. Later, Luke tells us that "all the believers were one in heart and mind."[9]

Notice that the Bible says *all*, not just some, came together in Christian community around one set of beliefs and convictions that were leading to a distinct set of actions and behaviors. In establishing a theology for Christian community, the apostle Paul writes, "There is one body and one Spirit—just as you were called to one hope when you were called—one Lord, one faith, one baptism; one God and Father of all, who is over all and through all and in all."[10] The distinct impression here is that embracing a common belief and purpose built on the teachings of Jesus and the apostles was, and still is, a requirement in order to be called a Christian community.

Most churches today have not been able to seize this simple idea of rallying around a common purpose because our culture of individualism does all in its power not to let it happen. Lyle Schaller, a leading church consultant over the past several decades, writes, "Rising from the debris of our lost values is the new value on the individual. The 'me' generation has given way to a 'me' world. The question is, how will the church, the ultimate 'we' organization, adjust?"[11]

Kenneth Kantzer, former professor at Trinity Evangelical Divinity School, made this prophetic statement based on his study of the modern church: "No church can be effective to bring clarity and commitment to a world when it is as ignorant of its own basic principles as is our church today. And unless we engage the church in a mighty program of reeducation, it will be unable to transmit a Christian heritage to its own children or to the society around it."[12]

In his article on the influence of individualism, Schaller goes on to ask, "So how do you build community? . . . The easiest way to consolidate a group is to give them a new common enemy. A more scripturally sound way is to develop shared experiences in support of a common cause."[13]

One of the most important writers of the twentieth century, C. S. Lewis, helps identify the common cause for Christians:

[Christ] works on us in all sorts of ways. . . . But above all, He works on us through each other. Men are mirrors, or "carriers" of Christ to other men. . . . Usually it is those who know Him that bring Him to others. That is why the Church, the whole body of Christians showing Him to one another, is so important. . . . It is easy to think that the Church has a lot of different objects—education, building, missions, holding services. . . . The Church exists for no other purpose but to draw men into Christ, to make them little Christs. If they are not doing that, all the cathedrals, clergy, missions, sermons, even the Bible itself, are simply a waste of time. God became Man for no other purpose. It is even doubtful, you know, whether the whole universe was created for any other purpose.[14]

Jesus himself gave us the mission to "make disciples" of people and to obey his entire teachings. Paul stated it this way: "My dear children, for whom I am again in the pains of childbirth until Christ is formed in you. . . ."[15]

What the church urgently needs to do is establish the biblical mission of seeing Christ formed in individuals as the foundational mission of biblical community. The second thing the church must do is define, as Dallas Willard has suggested, a "recognized, reasonable, theologically and psychologically sound approach to spiritual growth," or *Christ forming*.[16] We must adopt from the ancient church and redefine for the postmodern church what a follower of Christ looks like. Incorporating these common beliefs, practices, and virtues into the lives of people must constitute the central purpose that draws the Christian community together.

A word of caution here. The church must be careful not to confuse an assimilation strategy for church involvement with a spiritual formation model for community building. Both are necessary, but they are very different. An assimilation strategy defines how one gets involved in the life and programs of a church; a spiritual formation model defines the essential outcomes the church is attempting to get working into the lives of its members. Church leaders should first define the end objective for their people and then design an infrastructure to accomplish this in the lives of the people of the church. To have an effective assimilation strategy that will get people involved in the church but then to not have a clear idea of what the ultimate purpose of those structures are would be hollow and aimless. The Bible does not define church activities as "spiritual formation"; rather, spiritual growth involves the "renewing of the mind" in the core beliefs of the Christian faith.[17]

Central beliefs that forge our communion with God—such as our belief in the Trinity, salvation by grace, the authority of the Bible, the personal nature of God, and our identity in Christ—are a necessity. Central beliefs that cement our communion with people—such as our view of the church, biblical humanity, Christian compassion, eternity, and biblical stewardship—must be considered.

Spiritual growth involves practicing the ancient disciplines taught in the Bible and experienced throughout church history.[18] Christian disciplines that foster our relationship with God—such as worship, prayer, Bible study, and single-mindedness—should be included. The biblical practices of community, spiritual gifts, and giving away our time, money, faith, and even our life should be included to fulfill the royal law of loving our neighbor.

Of course, we should not forget to include in our common creed the basis of spiritual formation—the character of Christ.[19] When creating a common creed, it's hard to compete with the fruit of the Spirit: love, joy, peace, patience, kindness, goodness, faithfulness, gentleness, and self-control.

If Bob and Karen Johnson are going to satisfy their longing for more intimate relationships, they must find, and even help create, a Christian community where the *common mission* is to see individuals become fully developing followers of Christ. This community must have in place respected spiritual *authority*—individuals who are biblically literate and who can serve as exemplary spiritual mentors. This gathering must have a common *creed* that succinctly lays out the beliefs, practices, and virtues that the members of the community agree to follow, to encourage in each other, and to which they all are held accountable. They must resurrect old, or create new, Christian *traditions* that assist in cementing the history and purpose of the Christian faith for the next generation. And, if this community is to be effective long-term, there must be *standards* that are considered normal behavior for all followers of Christ.

Notice how Paul challenges the mind-set of individualism. If any of these characteristics are absent, the authenticity of the community will in some way be diminished:

> *If you have any encouragement from being united with Christ, if any comfort from his love, if any fellowship with the Spirit, if any tenderness and compassion, then make my joy*

complete by being like-minded, having the same love, being one in spirit and purpose. Do nothing out of selfish ambition or vain conceit, but in humility consider others better than yourselves. Each of you should look not only to your own interests, but also to the interests of others.

Your attitude should be the same as that of Christ Jesus.[20]

Whatever the model of spiritual formation, it should be promoted by the spiritual authority of the church, it should be taught at all levels, it should form a common language by which people of the community speak with each other, and it should be the benchmark against which we examine our lives as individuals and as a community.[21]

The church must ask itself the question, "What is our plan for teaching our people to obey everything Christ has commanded?" Dallas Willard challenges church leadership with this response:

The fact is that our existing churches and denominations do not have active, well-designed, intently pursued plans to accomplish this in their members. Just as you will not find any national leader today who has a plan for paying off the national debt; so you will not find any widely influential element of our church leadership that has a plan—not a vague wish or dream, but a plan—for implementing all phases of the Great Commission.[22]

A common purpose as defined by Scripture itself is what Bob and Karen—and all of us—need in order to experience Christian community. In the next chapter I'll take a look at what this might look like in real life.

5

REDISCOVERING BIBLICAL PURPOSE

Bob and Karen Johnson have been attending church services and church-sponsored activities for a while but have not had the opportunity to become part of a community of Christians focused on the same rich biblical purpose. This is true not only for the Johnsons but for most Christians today. As Dallas Willard puts it, paraphrasing G. K. Chesterton, "It's not so much that the Christian life has been tried and found wanting as it's never been tried at all."[1]

What you are about to read is one vision of what a community of faith might look when it gives people a real shot at experiencing our God-given purpose.

A WORD FROM JESUS

The sixty-six books of the Bible can be daunting and difficult for any person to get his or her arms around. It contains the beautiful story of God's plan to reconnect us to himself; it speaks clearly about the purpose of the church—to develop followers of Christ. However, the profile of a fully developing follower of Christ doesn't appear so simply defined within its pages, given the size and genre of the Bible. Even in Jesus' day, with the only reference being the thirty-nine books of the Old Testament, the people asked him to summarize the writings of Scripture. Jesus' answer began to form the operating system for living a religious life, as he divided God's will for holy living into two categories:

"Love the Lord your God with all your heart and with all your soul and with all your strength and with all your mind"; and, "Love your neighbor as yourself."²

Put simply, Jesus tells us that the first and foremost law of life is to love God. Flowing out of and motivated by our love for God is a love for others. There is a vertical dimension to our life (that is, loving God) and a horizontal dimension to our life (that is, loving our neighbor). A helpful way to understand Jesus' construction of the fulfilled life is to draw these two components to form the quadrant graph below:

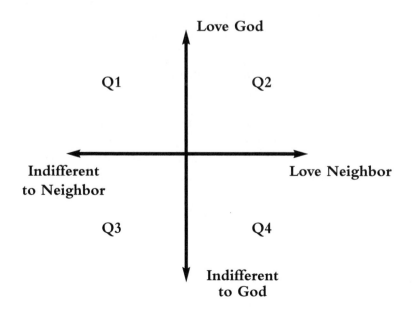

The objective of the Christian life is to reside in Quadrant 2, which entails that a person must both love God and love others. It is important to note that the thrust of the spiritual life in Christ is not to pursue our own individual happiness and fulfillment. Rather, we give ourselves to the pursuit of loving God and helping others. As a matter of fact, Jesus assumed that self-love comes rather naturally when he said we are to love our neighbor *as ourselves.* If we struggle with a lack of self-love and self-worth, the solution is not to focus all of our attention on loving ourselves. Jesus might even have chuckled at such a foreign suggestion. Instead, as we pursue the love of God and then turn and pour the substance of the love of God contained within us onto others, it brings meaning, significance, and contentment to our life.

Individualism taken to an extreme would land a person in Quadrant 3, a person indifferent to both God and others, absorbed in a selfish pursuit of personal gain. This is a dark, dreary, and lonely place to be—the place many people today have almost unconsciously adopted as their operating system for living.

Jesus shows the relationship of these two commandments in his teachings in John 15.

> *As the Father has loved me, so have I loved you. Now remain in my love. If you obey my commands, you will remain in my love, just as I have obeyed my Father's commands and remain in his love. I have told you this so that my joy may be in you and that your joy may be complete. My command is this: Love each other as I have loved you.* [3]

Jesus tells us that he loved us first and that we should seek to remain in this love by obeying his teachings.[4] His principal command is for us to love each other in the same way he has loved us. When we pour out on others Christ's love, which is embodied in us, it reinforces and strengthens the love we experience in our relationship with God. We learn here that loving God and loving each other are not mutually exclusive competencies. Rather, they feed off of and rely on each other to produce the end objective— becoming a disciple. What, then, do we get from all this "other focus"? Jesus said we get complete joy without ever pursuing it directly for ourselves.

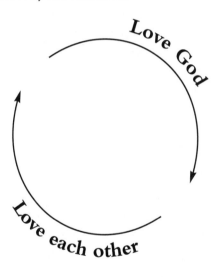

BUILDING ON THE TEACHINGS OF JESUS

The teachings of Jesus articulate the two broadest categories; thus, every command or principle for living found in the Bible can be placed under the broad umbrella of *loving God* or *loving others*. As we look at the instructions in the New Testament regarding loving others, we see a new distinction between loving those who are members of the body of Christ and those who are not. This expanded architecture should be kept in mind as we instruct people in the horizontal dimensions of Christian living.

As one reads from Genesis through Revelation, what are the common beliefs, practices, and virtues that have to do with loving God? What are the common beliefs, practices, and virtues that have to do with loving others? Thankfully, this is not the first time this important question has been asked; consequently, there is no need to develop a brand-new profile for becoming a disciple.

The thirty beliefs, practices, and virtues introduced on the next several pages form the foundation for what we call the Christian Life Profile (see pages 89–106 for a discussion of how to use the profile in creating true community).

Ancient Christian Beliefs

For centuries church leaders have read the Bible thoroughly and developed a list of dominant themes, by and large known only to the seminary-trained student as "systematic theology." Systematic theology is merely taking the most significant and recurring themes of the Bible and dropping them into separate buckets so we might assess each theme and learn from the comprehensive teachings on a particular subject. As we chew on these collective concepts around a single theme, they teach us how to think and live in a distinctively Christian way.

How might these ancient categories inform us of the essential beliefs of the Christian life today? Let's take a look.

- **Trinity** (Theology Proper, Christology, Pneumatology): the belief that the God of the Bible is the only true God—Father, Son, and Holy Spirit (see 2 Corinthians 13:14)
- **Salvation by Grace** (Soteriology): the belief that a person comes into a right relationship with God and is saved by his grace through faith in Jesus Christ (see Ephesians 2:8–9)
- **Authority of the Bible** (Bibliology): the belief that the Bible is the word of God and has the right to command our beliefs and actions (see 2 Timothy 3:16–17)
- **Personal God** (Transcendence, Immanence, Providence): the belief that God is involved in and cares about our daily lives (see Psalm 121)
- **Identity in Christ** (aspect of Sanctification): the belief that a person is significant because of his or her position as a child of God (see John 1:12–13)
- **Church** (Ecclesiology): the belief that the church is God's primary way to accomplish his purposes on earth today (see Ephesians 4:15–16)
- **Humanity** (Anthropology): the belief that all people are loved by God and need Jesus Christ as their Savior (see John 3:16)
- **Compassion** (aspect of Ecclesiology): the belief that God calls Christians to show compassion to those in need (see Psalm 82:3–4)
- **Eternity** (Eschatology): the belief that there is a heaven and a hell and that Jesus will return to judge

the earth and to establish his eternal kingdom (see John 14:1–4)

- **Stewardship** (aspect of Soteriology): the belief that everything a person owns belongs to God (see 1 Timothy 6:17–19)

There are certainly many other beliefs that could be identified, but these are the ones that have stood the test of time. Other key concepts, such as the doctrine of sin, can and should be taught under each category, particularly, in the core beliefs of *salvation by grace* and *humanity.* These core beliefs teach us who God is, how we come into a relationship with him, what he wants us to know and do, how he relates to us and is involved in our lives, and who we become when we know and love our God.

Our contemporary culture consists of the most educated people in all of human history, yet they are also the most biblically and spiritually illiterate. Researchers who keep their fingers on the pulse of America's spiritual culture, such as George Gallup Jr. and George Barna, have been warning us for years that our nation truly does experience this condition. George Gallup wrote the following:

> The churches of America face no greater challenge as we approach the next century than overcoming biblical illiteracy, and the prospects for doing so are formidable because the stark fact is, many Christians don't know what they believe or why. Our faith is not rooted in Scripture. We revere the Bible, but we don't read it. Some observers maintain that the Bible has not in any profound way penetrated our culture.[5]

George Barna has discovered that 82 percent of Americans believe that the Bible contains the words *God helps those who help themselves.*[6] The vast majority of people actually believe God is the founder of individualism! Speaking about the "postmodern person" who has a hunger for ancient spiritual truths and biblical community, Dieter and Valerie Zander write, "Many postmodern people do not have any residual understanding of the triune God and his story. To assume that they do is deadly to anyone who wants to communicate with them. But anyone who will drop that assumption and tell the story of the God who searches out the lost will find a curious audience waiting."[7] Here we learn that though one hungers for the knowledge of God, just being hungry doesn't mean one has tasted and digested it.

The goal is not for a person to believe that these core concepts are the only right answers; nor is the goal a mere cognitive exchange of information about doctrine, although that's not a bad place to start. The goal is the *renewing of the mind.*[8] It is important for followers of Christ to have their thinking so saturated in these truths through meditation and experience that it forms and informs both the way they see and live life.[9]

Here is a significant question to ponder: Can a group of people be classified as a Christian community when they are as ignorant of the core beliefs that have to do with loving God and loving neighbor as our present-day culture is? What would it be like to gather in a community of faith where the people were committed to growing "in the grace and knowledge of our Lord and Savior Jesus Christ"?[10]

Ancient Christian Practices

Throughout its history the Christian faith has regarded a specific collection of spiritual practices, or disciplines, as essential for growth toward Christlikeness. These ancient practices emerge from the pages of Scripture. They do not equal spiritual growth any more than the core beliefs do. They do assist us, however, in getting into the workroom of the Holy Spirit, where he can transform us.

Looking again at John 15, we can make the clear connection from the practices of loving each other to abiding, or remaining, in God's love. These daily disciplines are motivated by the core beliefs. For example, because I believe that God is involved in and cares about my daily life, I practice praying to him, knowing that he hears me. While there are several ways to list and label these spiritual practices, consider the following ten:

- **Worship**: worshiping God for who he is and what he has done for us (see Psalm 95:1–7)
- **Prayer**: praying to God to know him, to lay our requests before him, and to find direction for our daily life (see Psalm 66:16–20)
- **Bible Study**: reading the Bible to know God, to hold to the truth, and to find direction for our daily life (see Hebrews 4:12)
- **Single-Mindedness**: focusing on God and his priorities for our life (see Matthew 6:33)
- **Biblical Community**: fellowshipping with other Christians to fulfill God's purposes in our life, in others' lives, and in the world (see Acts 2:42–47)

- **Spiritual Gifts**: using the gifts God has given us to fulfill God's purposes (see 1 Corinthians 12:1–31)
- **Giving Away Our Time**: giving away our time to fulfill God's purposes (see Colossians 3:17)
- **Giving Away Our Money**: giving away our money to fulfill God's purposes (see 2 Corinthians 8:7)
- **Giving Away Our Faith**: giving away our faith to fulfill God's purposes (see Ephesians 6:19–20)
- **Giving Away Our Life**: giving away our life to fulfill God's purposes (see Romans 12:1–2)

Can you imagine the net result of a group of Christians who were all committed to practicing these disciplines in an increasing measure as they fellowshipped together? What difference it would make if just a small group of men and women would ask to be held mutually accountable to "practice" the Christian faith! How many lives would be transformed into a greater Christlikeness if these disciplines were not practiced merely by isolated individuals but by a common, committed gathering of Christ-followers! The implications are staggering.

Ancient Christian Virtues

The Christian beliefs deal with what we need to *know*. The Christian practices deal with what we need to *do*. The final area of consideration is Christian virtues, or what we need to *be*—the ultimate expression of Christlikeness.

As with our core beliefs and practices, there is no need for fresh thinking in this area—just fresh obedience. The New Testament is filled with listings of the virtues God wants to see developed in us as a result of the work of the Holy Spirit.[11] Pause to consider for a moment the incredible impact these virtues would have if commonly embraced as the goal and the customary lifestyle for the followers of Christ in a Christian community.

- **Joy**: having inner contentment and purpose in spite of our circumstances (see John 15:11)
- **Peace**: being free from anxiety because things are right between God and me, and between me and others (see Philippians 4:6–7)
- **Faith(fulness)**: being faithful to fulfill God's will for our life (see Proverbs 3:3–4)
- **Self-Control**: having the power to control ourselves (see 1 Thessalonians 5:6)
- **Love**: unconditionally loving others (see 1 John 4:10–12)
- **Patience**: being patient with others (see Proverbs 14:29)
- **Kindness/Goodness**: choosing to consistently do the right thing in our relationships with others (see 1 Thessalonians 5:15)
- **Gentleness**: being thoughtful, considerate, and calm as we deal with others (see Philippians 4:5)
- **Humility**: choosing to esteem others above ourselves (see Philippians 2:3–4)
- **Hope**: coping with the hardships of life and death because of the hope we have in Jesus Christ (see Hebrews 6:17–20)

DOES IT REALLY MATTER?

The question the well-bred American pragmatist would ask is, "Does all this really make a difference?" The answer is most definitely yes! Consider a study conducted by George Gallup Jr., who randomly polled a cross section of people regarding their feelings about twelve Christian beliefs and practices.[12] He then asked a series of follow-up questions about Christian virtues, such as experiencing joy, forgiving others who deeply hurt you, and showing compassion. His findings were shocking. Those who said they strongly embraced these twelve beliefs and practices showed a significant increase in personal joy, the ability to forgive others, and a willingness to show compassion when compared to the people who said they strongly disagreed with these beliefs and practices. When the Christian life is tried, it works!

PURPOSES OF BIBLICAL COMMUNITY

If Bob and Karen were to join a small gathering of Christians committed to developing as individuals in the above areas (or in a substantive biblical alternative), what would that group do? Essentially, they would focus internally on helping each other within the community to grow in their love for God and for neighbor. Externally, the gathering of disciples would work together to love others outside of the group, as Christ would have them do. Let me suggest the following covenant as a working model to bring it all together. To make it easier to remember, it conveniently forms the acronym S - E - R -V - I - C - E.

SEVEN FUNCTIONS OF BIBLICAL COMMUNITY

A Covenant

S Spiritual Formation

As members of a biblical community, we will annually assess our own development in Christ, using the Christian Life Profile. We will then confess our areas of struggles to one another and set personal goals for our growth in Christ in the year to come. Through the year we will share our progress and encourage one another monthly in our pursuit of Christlikeness.

E Evangelism

Each household within the biblical community will commit to pray for at least three households within their neighborhood who need to embrace the gospel of Jesus Christ. As a biblical community we will pray together monthly for the personal requests of these neighbors. We will hold one another accountable to prayerfully reach out to these families. We desire to see at least one household come to faith in Christ each year.

R Reproduction

Each biblical community is open to welcoming new members and will have at least one "leader in training" who is preparing to launch a new group as the Lord adds to their number. We will seek to reproduce another group at least once a year.

V Volunteerism

As members of the biblical community we will commit ourselves to support the greater body of Christ at our local church through involvement in ministries and service opportunities such as youth, children, worship, ushers, and greeters. We will celebrate what God is doing in the greater body of Christ through a special quarterly gathering.

I International Missions

As an expression of our desire to share Christ with the world, the biblical community will support at least one international missions project through increased awareness, commitment to prayer, financial contributions, and hands-on involvement.

C Care

The foundation of biblical community will be our commitment to care for one another. This will be manifested in practical help for those in difficult and crisis situations—hospital or home visits, meal preparation, prayer, referral to church and community resources, and the like.

E Extending Compassion

In response to the social needs of our community, each biblical community will commit to participating as families in at least four on-site compassion projects throughout the year. Monthly, the biblical community will select, prepare for, or celebrate their involvement in their compassion project.

These biblical functions are not departments within the church that people pick and choose. Rather, they are a singular relational gathering committed to embrace together all of the seven functions. This will require that the church not develop competing activities or functions *at* the church but rather allow the small group members to simplify their church lives by means of this one group.

Some might say that seven functions are too much. Not really. All of these functions are required of the members of the body of Christ. There isn't a great deal of fluff here. Parceling out each of these functions into separate departments in the church doesn't make it easier for the individual in the end; it seems only to make it harder. Having a different set of relationships for each function not only takes more time to manage and implement, but diminishes the opportunity to really get to know anyone well. Having these essential purposes of the church centered in one relational gathering causes the members to grow deep in their love for each other as they struggle together to do God's work.

Of course, this doesn't mean that every member of the group will do everything. Rather, each activity will call on different people to exercise different gifts within the group.[13] Those who are organized will organize. Those who are endowed with an extra measure of hospitality will show hospitality. Those who are intercessors will cover the group's activities in effective prayer. Those who have an extra container of mercy will pour it out on the troubled soul inside or outside the group. Those who have unique talents and resources will offer up these gifts as a sacrifice of praise to help fulfill the call to be the church. Those who are skilled in craftsmanship will make or repair what is needed (the mechanic, for example, will fix the car of the single mother). While everyone contributes financial gifts to care for the poor, the one to whom God has given much will ensure that the need is met. Christ never intended for everyone to do all the work. Instead, as each one does his or her part, the body grows and is built up, and the work of God gets done.[14]

Jesus once declared that those around us will know we are his disciples by our love for one another.[15] Consider this: In a culture of individualism, when do non-Christians get to see other Christians loving each other in such a way that it compels *them* to run to Jesus Christ? The church has all too often mirrored the culture by making Christianity an individual sport. In our current small group structure, we tend to huddle together with other Christians and care for each other and pray for each other—but the non-Christian never gets to see any of this. If we do engage in sharing our faith, we typically do it one-on-one, isolated from the life of loving Christian community. Or perhaps those with the gift of evangelism gather together, strategize, and then go out to confront individuals one-on-one with the gospel—as though their method of words could possibly be a better method than Jesus' idea of community evangelism.

The late Francis Schaeffer gave us the gift of these rich words: "Our relationship with each other is the criterion the world uses to judge whether our message is truthful—Christian community is the final apologetic."[16]

What the Johnson family needs to do is to become a part of a Christian community that has a qualified spiritual authority. They need to be part of a collection of individuals who are functionally competent in the teachings of Scripture and who model these teachings in daily life. They need to belong to a Christian community that embraces together a common creed that is biblical, substantive, and practical. The group should have traditions that ensure that this way of life is being passed down to the next generation. Each member should openly and freely commit to being accountable to the rest of the members of the group—to live by standards that are the norm for Christian living and that flow from the common creed and the Scriptures. In the final analysis, Bob, Karen, and their two children need to belong to a Christian community that has a common mission. Eberhard Arnold, founder of the Bruderhof Communities, writes, "The more clearly a community defines its unique task, the more deeply conscious it must be of the *Una Sancta,* the one Church."[17]

If you are a pastor, a church leader, or someone who is responsible for building community, you may be wondering how to implement these principles in a church. The next chapter will discuss this very concern by describing how one church, Pantego Bible Church, has tackled the implementation.

6

IMPLEMENTING A COMMON PURPOSE

If you've ever visited the city of London and traveled on the Underground, you no doubt remember that every time a railcar pulls up and the doors open, a woman's voice would say, "Mind the gap." This, of course, is referring to the gap that exists between the platform and the threshold of the railcar. The last thing you want to do is fall into the gap! Pastors and church leaders need to continually implore members of their congregation to "mind the gap." The spiritual gap is the chasm between where we are right now in our spiritual journey and where we need to be as we seek to become more like Christ.

As a pastor I've been challenged by Bob Buford to take a hard look at how a church measures its success. Bob is a successful Christian businessman and the author of the best-selling book *Halftime*.[1] Through an organization he founded called Leadership Network, he has done much to help pastors examine tough issues and learn how to innovate in a biblical way.

Bob Buford has convinced me that whatever we measure is really our mission. At Pantego Bible Church our only measurement at the time was the ABCs (attendance, buildings, and cash). Therefore, regardless of the platitudes offered up in bulletins and letterheads, our mission was to add more people to our membership who give more money so we can build bigger buildings to contain even more people, who can give more money, and so on and so on. Most people would deny that this is true of their church, but if the ABCs are the only valid measurement points, it is really more true than we want to believe. As a matter of fact, job security for most pastors comes more from numerical growth than from spiritual growth. The reality of this whole matter disgusted me as I pondered the purity of my motives for going into pastoral ministry in the first place. I got in the game of pastoral ministry because I truly wanted to see people experience the life of Christ in them. Most days in "the ministry" have nothing to do with this.

I decided to take Buford up on his challenge and define a biblically based measurement barometer for the local church. One of the most prevalent mistakes I saw among those who wanted to break away from the numerical-monitoring grind of head count, square footage, and cash was this: the attempt to pawn off an assimilation strategy as spiritual formation. What happens is that instead of taking attendance at the worship services only, we now take it at other church-sponsored events, such as small groups and seminars. The assumption is that if people are attending these additional events they must be growing. The most clever and orderly churches organize these events in a recommended

sequence—"do this first, this second, this third, and so forth."
An assimilation plan for church involvement beyond the
worship service is actually very good and absolutely essential, but it does not equal, nor does it necessarily enhance,
spiritual formation. Why not? Robert Wuthnow shares from
his research that most small group experiences do not esteem
the value of accountability. The ones that do typically focus
not so much on spiritual life goals as on personal growth
goals, such as weight loss or career advancement. The truth
is, many small groups degenerate into social groups within
six months, with just a token prayer offered at mealtime.
Here's what I'm trying to say: You can have 100 percent participation in church-sponsored small groups, but it doesn't
necessarily mean that the people in these groups are becoming more like Christ.

The development of the Christian Life Profile, introduced in the last chapter, was a breakthrough for our
church. When an effective and efficient assimilation strategy (one that includes small groups) is used to move people
along in these core beliefs, practices, and virtues, spiritual
development can really take place.

DEFINING A DISCIPLE

The first step you must take toward creating community and implementing your common purpose is to decide
that the central mission of the church is to develop disciples. This mission should be captured in an official statement and should be promoted everywhere. It should be
printed on everything you put into print, but it doesn't stop
there.

The second step is to define the outcome of a disciple—to lay out the content that forms the common purpose of community. To help us do this, we have introduced a profile established from the summary statement Jesus made in his response to the question about how to inherit eternal life—Love God/Love Neighbor (see pages 71–80).[2] Each of the ten beliefs, ten practices, and ten virtues contributes significantly to our love for God and our love for each other. We were fortunate to have the assistance of many people inside, and particularly outside, our church as we developed this profile over the course of a four-year period. George Gallup Jr. and Timothy Jones's book, *The Saints Among Us,* was particularly helpful in giving us insight into Christian beliefs, practices, and virtues. Moreover, we had the great advantage of getting detailed feedback from such kingdom contributors as Dallas Willard, J. I. Packer, George Barna, Larry Crabb, and several others.

Feel free to adopt our definition, adjust it, or even to start from scratch. If you start from scratch, the key question you will want to ask is this: What does the Bible describe as the core characteristics of a fully developing follower of Christ? If the mission of the church is to make disciples, and you define a disciple in very specific terms, then it only makes sense that the church be structured in such a way that these specific areas will be incorporated into the lives of people who attend your church. In other words, the church leadership must be fully devoted to developing church members into fully devoted disciples.

Once the basic structure of the profile has been set, you should not tamper with it continually or make numerous changes to it. Experts suggest that it takes about three years for a language to become part of a culture. If you keep changing your definitions and the details of the profile, you essentially start the three-year clock over again. It has taken three full years for our definition of a disciple and the language that accompanies it to become a part of the corporate culture of our church. (And there were times along the way when we wondered if anyone would get it.)

It is also helpful to develop creedal, or affirmation, statements to accompany each item of your profile—which will provide more meat to the bones of the skeleton. For example, if one of the components of your profile is *the authority of the Bible,* you may want to have a statement that will take the basic idea to the next level: "We believe the Bible is the word of God and has the right to command our beliefs and actions." It's also crucial for you to identify at least one central passage of Scripture that supports each area.

INTENTIONAL LEVELS OF COMMUNITY

Once you have defined what a disciple is, you must identify the vehicles or strategies you will use to build the aspects of the Christian Life Profile into the lives of the people in your church. This is your assimilation plan. It is the delivery system for the outcomes you desire for your members. Biblical community cannot be limited to the small group experience but must extend to the full experience of life together in the body of Christ. Therefore, every aspect of the church must be developed with the notion in mind that we are the community of faith in Christ united in our mission to make disciples. We have identified four distinct, integrated levels of involvement for the people of our church that will help activate the Christian Life Profile in their lives. All four levels of relationships contribute to what it means to be part of a vibrant biblical community. They can be viewed like a funnel.

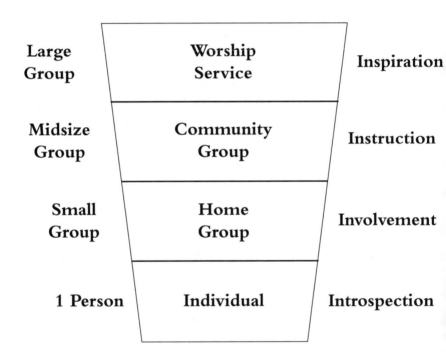

INTENTIONAL ASSIMILATION STRATEGY

Large Group	Worship Service	Inspiration
Midsize Group	Community Group	Instruction
Small Group	Home Group	Involvement
1 Person	Individual	Introspection

Let's take a closer look at each of these levels of relationship:

Worship Service: The purpose of the worship service is to inspire *people to become fully developing followers of Christ*

In our worship, the Christian Life Profile can be seen as providing scope and sequence, serving as the basis for our curriculum. We needed to develop a systematic way to teach these principles to our congregation. Drawing on the historical concept of the church calendar, we created what we call *The Spiritual Formation Calendar.* Instead of the calendar being predominantly doctrinal in nature, our calendar is driven by the goal of spiritual formation. We have systematically placed all essential beliefs, practices, and virtues into a fifty-two-week schedule (see appendix).

Each week we focus on a particular aspect of the profile of a disciple. Each year we take a different angle and use a different biblical passage to teach these principles to our congregation. When we come to the end of the calendar year, we start again. Because we've been doing this now for over three years, the language we use in building our profile of a disciple is beginning to emerge as a corporate language for spiritual growth.

For example, in the first year we did a series on the Trinity called *Contact: Exploring God.* We studied the concepts of God's existence, identity, and personality, using such passages as Psalm 63, John 1, and John 17. In the second year we did another study on the Trinity called *Empowered Living: Tapping into the Power of the Holy Spirit,* in which we explored the work of the Holy Spirit in the spiritual transformation process as taught in Romans 8. In the third year we did still another series on the Trinity called *Trusting God: Holding On to God's Goodness in the Face of Life's Trials*. Here we probed the attribute of God's goodness, mining the treasures found in Psalm 145, John 9, and 2 Corinthians 12.

These intentional series form the focus of our worship service. I (or someone on our pastoral team) preach the sermon. Everything in the service, from the music to the reciting of the creed to a live testimony, seeks to *embed* these biblical ideas in the gathering of Christians and seekers and *inspire* them with these core beliefs, practices, and virtues. We want to be content-driven as opposed to style-driven. We have tried to provide a model anyone can use, no matter whether your church is contemporary or traditional.

Our philosophy of preaching is built on a three-prong approach: theological, biblical, and relevant. The *theological* aspect is our definition of a disciple and our formulation of the essential beliefs, practices, and virtues of the Christian Life Profile. We are developing a theology for each of these categories, using all sixty-six books of the Bible. This theology is not designed to stay within the walls of a seminary classroom but is intended to form an operating system for Christian living.

In addition, each message flows from a particular *biblical* text, with the integrity of the historical and literary context, as well as the author's intent, maintained and developed. For example, if we were to teach about the death of Sarah from the text of Genesis 23, we would not focus on the subject of grief and grief recovery, even though this is a useful and practical topic. Why not?

Because it wasn't the intended meaning of this text. Rather, we would accentuate the theological topic, the virtue of faithfulness. This passage highlights Abraham's faith that God would one day give his people the land of Canaan. Burying Sarah in Canaan before the people possessed the land demonstrated Abraham's faithfulness in believing that God would keep his promise. By all means, the topic of grief needs to be taught, but not by using this passage as the focal point. The power of the message is in communicating the inspired Word of God. If we want our messages to be inspiring and to transform lives, then we must maintain the integrity of the inspired text.

Finally, our preaching must be *relevant*. We not only seek to interpret the Scriptures but also the culture we live in and minister to. We look for the point of intersection between ancient biblical times and contemporary times. In the case of Genesis 23, the application to contemporary living is powerful. It can be summarized in this important question: What do we need to do today to demonstrate that we believe God will keep his promises to us in the future?

This method has reenergized my preaching ministry with balance and purpose. Whenever one of these three aspects is emphasized in isolation from the other two, something crucial is lost. Whenever biblical exposition is done without the theological foundations and the link to present-day living, it is difficult for people to grasp how your exposition correlates to what you have taught in the past and how it affects the issues people face today. I know of people who have listened to Bible teachers for decades and yet do not have a practical and holistic understanding of how the Christian life works. By the same token, if preachers seek to be relevant apart from the theological teachings and biblical exposition, they stand in danger of scratching where the people itch but doing so with *human* teaching and wisdom, not with the profound and transformational revelation of God.[3] In my opinion, this is the way many contemporary churches have built large congregations. We have series after series on marriage, relationships, parenting, finances, and success—each of them being important topics that deal with the questions people are asking—but often our treatment of the subject resembles more the teaching found in the Self-Help/Motivation section of Barnes and Noble than it does a thoughtful presentation of Scripture.

Teaching from *The Spiritual Formation Calendar* forces me to bring balance to my teaching ministry. Each year I am required to teach biblical topics that have not been on too many top-ten lists in the last twenty-five years. Topics such as the Trinity, eternity, the doctrine of the church, and total commitment to God are seen as uninteresting or irrelevant by many church attendees. The burden is on me to show how these weighty topics *are* relevant to everyday life in a manner that is accurate and appealing. I personally thrive on this challenge, as do, I believe, most who have been called to preach.

Our goal is that when people walk out of the worship service each Sunday, they will be inspired to suit up for another exciting week of intentional faith-pursuit centered in Jesus Christ. On our team we have a little saying that goes like this: "People won't perspire in their faith Monday through Saturday if they are not inspired in their faith on Sunday." This is the intentional aim of the worship service, as we work to apply the Christian Life Profile in all its facets to the community of faith under our care.

Community Group: The purpose of the Community Group is to instruct *people to become fully developing followers of Christ*

The second level of intentional discipleship through community is the midsize group, which we call the *Community Group*. While the purpose of the worship service is to *inspire* people in all the facets of the Christian Life Profile, the purpose of the Community Group is to *instruct* people in the profile.

While many contemporary churches do not have a midsize group experience, we find this to be the most efficient and effective way to achieve our biblical educational objectives. This task can be transferred to the small group, but in our experience there are at least two negatives in doing so. First, the midsize group is made up of about fifty individuals; the small group is made up of about ten individuals. To transfer education to the small group means you must recruit and train five times the number of qualified teachers as you would if you carried out your teaching in the midsize group. Second, if the small group is used for education, it minimizes the level of intimacy you can achieve and the opportunity for experiential involvement so accessible in the small group. We have observed some churches that have offered the "midsize experience" but not the small group experience. Here too the same problem can emerge—trying to stuff two different functions (instruction and intimacy) into one container. Because of this, we have found the dual infrastructure of the midsize and the small-size group to work best in accomplishing the overall mission of the church.

The Community Group is the place where relationships and community begin to form for the individual. The first step people are encouraged to take after attending our worship service is to become part of a midsize group of people who all live in their neighborhood or surrounding area. While the Community Group has a life beyond a Sunday gathering, our central meeting time is Sunday morning on the church campus. It is out of this relational group that everything we want to accomplish as a church will flow. Instead of creating multiple relational worlds to manage in the church—with all kinds of relationships that never go deep—we encourage people to make this gathering of people central to their life and spiritual development. In part 2, I'll explain in detail why we group our people geographically.

You may be wondering what these midsize groups that gather on a Sunday do with their time. The purpose of the Sunday morning experience is education, that is, instruction in the core beliefs, practices, and virtues of the Christian life. We prepare study guides for each message and series presented at our worship services. Members of Community Groups pick up the guides from our Resource Booth, download them from our Web site, or receive them by e-mail each week. Throughout the week they study the lesson, and then on Sunday they come to the worship service and, we hope, are inspired. Following the service they attend their Community Group, where a teacher/facilitator leads a discussion on the subject. The personal study they have done during the week fuels the discussion. The discussion in the Community Group provides a "breakout" from the worship service and an outlet to share what they have learned in their personal study. It is our firm belief that drilling down three times with three different types of educational experiences on one topic produces better results than three disconnected educational experiences on three different topics.

Home Group: The purpose of Home Group is to involve *people in the Seven Functions of Biblical Community*

The focus of the Home Group is *involvement*. Our primary strategy is not to offer another Bible study but rather to encourage the practice of the Christian life in community. The primary practices are laid out in a covenant that involves a commitment to seven purposes or functions of biblical community (see pages 82–83). The fifty people who gather in the midsize Community Group now seek to go to another level of commitment and intimacy by forming five groups of ten people that meet in homes throughout the week (primarily on Sunday nights). Note that we're not seeking to add new relationships to the equation but rather to deepen the ones already developing as a result of the Community Group.

The first goal is for the members of the Home Group to function in interdependent relationships, assisting each other in growth toward Christlikeness, as defined by the Christian Life Profile. Each member enters the group committed to his or her own growth in Christ, as well as to helping the other group members grow in Christ. This goal is facilitated in a very simple way. We have designed an assessment tool based on the Christian Life Profile (see pages 74–80 for a list of the thirty common beliefs, practices, and virtues that make up the Christian Life Profile). Essentially, this assessment tool helps group members identify one to three areas of the profile they will personally focus on in the upcoming year. They share these results with the rest of the group members, who in turn agree to pray for and support them in this targeted pursuit of Christian growth.

The second goal is for Home Group members to practice their growing faith by reaching out to others outside the group, as defined in the SERVICE covenant mentioned above. As a fully functioning biblical community, the group together plans and carries out evangelism in the neighborhood, extends compassion to the local community, and supports the work of international missions throughout the world. These functions, which are typically centralized in many churches within departments set up in a committee structure, are decentralized within all our Home Groups. While a centralized structure is cleaner and easier to operate, in the end it more resembles the way a business is run than a dynamic community, which the church is called to be. The decentralized model stretches the gifts of the body, produces more ownership among a broader group of people, and accomplishes more in the end than could be done with a handful of committee members. In addition, this model of community achieves our stated conviction that we want first of all to organize people around relationships and then allow the functional purposes to flow from these relationships, instead of organizing people around the functional purposes and expect meaningful relationships and community to emerge. In chapter 14 I'll explain in more detail how the Home Group accomplishes its functions of evangelism, social compassion, and international missions.

Individual: The purpose for each individual is to be introspective *about his or her personal growth as a fully developing follower of Christ*

The end of the funnel comes down to the individual and his or her relationship with God. While the individual must never be viewed in isolation from the biblical community (participants in the worship service, the Community Group, and the Home Group), there is a responsibility each individual has as a fully functioning member of the community. We ask each member (as long as they've willfully agreed to make the commitment) to evaluate his or her life in relationship to the facets of the Christian Life Profile.

I mentioned on the previous page that we've created a tool that helps each individual assess where he or she stands in relationship to the benchmarks of the Christian Life Profile. The intent is that every member would complete this assessment once a year in the context of the Home Group. We feel strongly that the process of introspection is not only enhanced but also legitimized when done in the context of a safe, loving, and mutually accountable fellowship of believers.

We would like to see every member of a Home Group personally interact with the Christian Life Profile by selecting one belief or practice and one virtue they will focus on for the given year. Once a desired area of growth is selected, we supply a list of resources (by category) that are intended to help the member move toward personal transformation. We know that consuming the resources doesn't equal life transformation, but it does create potential movement toward it. The resources may be books, audiotapes, videotapes, or CD-ROM programs; some are a variety of classes to attend, some are spiritual disciplines to practice, and the like. Our church has a resource center that stocks most of these items for people to conveniently purchase. Recommending the best practical resources for spiritual growth is becoming one of the new roles church leaders can play on behalf of their members in light of the twenty-first century "information overload" age.

The *worship service,* the *Community Group,* the *Home Group,* and the *individual* represent four levels of integrated involvement. There are different functions at each level, based on the size of the gathering—all united around the goal of accomplishing the single mission of the church, namely, to make disciples. Each stage of involvement contributes something unique to the process of disciple making. When a visitor comes to our church, we sit down with them and explain our mission and define the levels of involvement designed to achieve the mission in their life. The first gathering with new people is called *Newcomers' Coffee.* New people gather one Sunday morning a month to be introduced to the mission and structure of the church. Those who are ready to commit to the next level go to our *New Member Class,* which further instructs them in how our church works. This method ensures that new people are informed of what we are trying to accomplish and how we intend to accomplish it in their lives.

CHILDREN AND YOUTH MINISTRIES

In a nutshell, what I have just described as our intentional strategy to move adults toward Christlikeness is the same strategy we use for our children and youth. The worship services for children and youth are designed around their development stage and include the music and learning styles that facilitate their growth. We have worship services designed for children, first grade through fourth grade, fifth and sixth grade, seventh and eighth grade, and ninth through twelfth grade. In addition, our children and young people work from the same *Spiritual Formation Calendar* (see appendix) as the adults, but we tailor the content and application to meet their needs. So every Sunday after the service and morning activities have concluded, when the family gets in the car together to go home, everyone can talk about the same aspect of Christian development. You have to experience it in order to feel the power of the concept.

Both the children and young people have midsize gatherings. The children's midsize program, which is equivalent to the adult Community Group, meets during the first and third hour on Sunday morning, while their worship service is at the middle hour. The youth ministries conduct their midsize groups on Wednesday evenings. The purpose of the midsize group experience for children and youth is the same as for the adult Community Groups—*instruction* in the various facets of the Christian Life Profile.

Children and youth participate in our Home Group structure as a crucial component of community. Many church models integrate children and youth at the worship service level but then segregate them at the midsize and small group level. We have determined to do just the opposite, as indicated by the graph below.

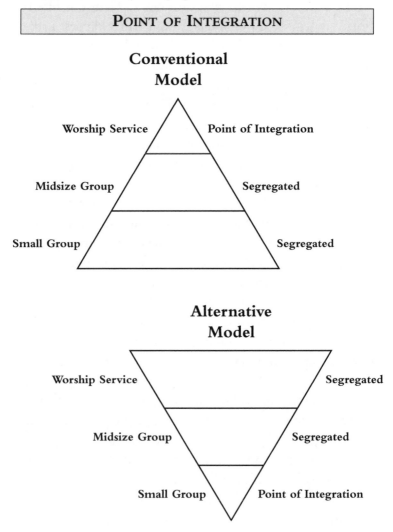

POINT OF INTEGRATION

Conventional Model

Worship Service — Point of Integration

Midsize Group — Segregated

Small Group — Segregated

Alternative Model

Worship Service — Segregated

Midsize Group — Segregated

Small Group — Point of Integration

We have distinct worship services and midsize groups for children and youth on Sunday morning and Wednesday night, but we include them with the adults at the Home Group level. People will have varying opinions about this concept, but we have found that it makes the most sense, given our convictions about community. Notice I didn't say it was easier or more convenient! In chapters 10 and 14 I will explain more about this decision and how it works in practice.

FEEDBACK LOOPS AND PLANNING

Remember this nugget of wisdom? *The church sets goals in those areas they can measure.* For years the church has only had the ABCs of ministry as "feedback loops"—attendance, buildings, and cash. If we agree that these three things are only resources and not the mission itself, then we must find a way to get feedback on how well we are doing at accomplishing our mission. For us, our mission can be cautiously and yet tangibly measured by the feedback our members give us on where they are in relation to the Christian Life Profile and the Seven Functions of Biblical Community. We are able to take quarterly and annual snapshots of our congregation by means of surveying them on a particular Sunday or weekday, and then using the information in our evaluation and planning meetings so that we can focus our goals on the spiritual development of the congregation. The dream is for this kind of information to be brought to every annual planning retreat. If the members of our congregation are struggling with biblical literacy, personal prayer, or self-control, then we need to make intentional plans to help them grow in these areas.

As I uncover two additional obstacles to community, and the two solutions that can help us overcome these obstacles, I'll also provide insight into how these solutions affect our infrastructure and the strategy we use to accomplish the mission of making disciples in the context of authentic community (see chapters 10 and 14). While this chapter focused on how we might instill a common purpose within the church as an essential component to biblical community, there is so much more to discover. Please continue to read on!

PART 2

CONNECTING TO A COMMON PLACE

7

THE PROBLEM OF ISOLATION

It can never be said that Adele Gaboury's neighbors were less than responsible.

When her front lawn grew hip-high, they had a local boy mow it down. When her pipes froze and burst, they had the water turned off. When the mail spilled out the front door, they called the police. The only thing they didn't do was check to see if she was alive.

She wasn't.

On Monday, police climbed her crumbling brick stoop, broke in the side door of her little blue house, and found what they believe to be the seventy-three-year-old woman's skeletal remains sunk in a five-foot-high pile of trash, where they had apparently lain, perhaps for as long as four years.

"It's not really a very friendly neighborhood," said Eileen Dugan, seventy, once a close friend of

Gaboury's, whose house sits less than twenty feet from the dead woman's home. "I'm as much to blame as anyone. She was alone and needed someone to talk to, but I was working two jobs and I was sick of her coming over at all hours. Eventually I stopped answering the door."[1]

Isolation. It's the second major obstacle to connecting in true community. This contemporary human condition flows out of the first major obstacle, namely, a culture of individualism, which promises to give us the best—only to inflict on us the disease of loneliness.

Remember the Johnson family? They have the same problem, even though it has certainly not manifested itself as severely as it did in the life of Adele Gaboury. They are not yet aware of their problem as something that robs them of community, for it's usually not recognized until trouble hits. But they clearly have the disease. All you have to do is look back at chapter 1 to see how isolated Bob and Karen are and just how little time they have to do anything about it.

How did two highly educated, intelligent people get themselves into this place? Well, it wasn't so much a situation they consciously chose to adopt as it was something they were drawn into—like many of us are. Just as they were influenced by a culture of individualism, so they were influenced by a culture of isolation. As it turned out, the Johnsons were simply mimicking the lifestyles of the people they admired from a distance; they came down with the same thing these people had been afflicted with— "closet loneliness"—a type of isolation that can't readily be seen in public but is nonetheless very real and very painful.

A MODERN-DAY PRISON

When did this experience of isolation begin to rear its ugly head against the American people? Once again sociology experts point to the 1950s as a pivotal period in the development of a culture of isolation. It was during this era that Americans began to build places to live that have turned out to be more of a prison than a home—we know these places as *the suburbs. Fort Worth Star-Telegram* staff writer Liz Stevens writes the following:

> Suburbs were created after World War II to remedy a housing shortage where the land was the cheapest. The automobile made it easy for people to commute longer distances to work. The clean, spacious suburbs, as they were, fit neatly into the concept of the American Dream. What happened is that suburban developers created a housing market aimed at newly affluent populations. That, plus deteriorating inner-city services (especially schools), racism, and other factors, catalyzed the white middle-class's flight to the "burbs." But these developers were not architects or urban planners, and the new suburbs did not take into account basic human needs.[2]

What did suburban design, or lack of design, do to keep our most basic needs from being met? Consider life in community before the 1950s. In ancient communities, including those built in America prior to the 1950s, designers placed residences, retail stores, and workplaces within walking distance of each other—and they did this, for the most part, for purely practical reasons. The kind of individualized transportation available to people today via the automobile was not available to prior generations. Yet, as it turns out, these densely created communities met more than practical needs; as a result of their layout, they facilitated our more basic and essential *relational* needs as well.

Paul Geisel, a professor of urban affairs at the University of Texas at Arlington, writes:

> Before suburbs, developers would build on city streets already laid out for them. In a typical pre-World War II urban neighborhood, homes were built upward to promote density and placed close to the street. They had spacious, covered front porches close to the public sidewalk, making it easy to talk with neighbors walking back from the local market. Today's subdivisions feature wide, winding streets, which promote speedy driving. New homes with tiny front porches sit imposingly behind large private lawns. And there is no corner store, or public space for community gatherings.[3]

Nan Ellin, assistant professor of urban design and planning at the University of Cincinnati, adds to Geisel's indictment by pointing out that all you have in the suburbs is private space. People drive into their driveways, go into their houses, and never see one another. And when television and newspapers become a person's only source of information about his or her community, fear and isolation run rampant.[4]

Philip Langdon, senior editor at *Progressive Architecture* magazine, observes the following:

> The United States has become a predominantly suburban nation, but not a very happy one. . . . It is no coincidence that at the moment when the United States has become a predominantly suburban nation, the

country has suffered a bitter harvest of individualized trauma, family distress, and civic decay.[5]

Writing for the *Atlantic Monthly,* author James Howard Kunstler is brutal to the suburban way of life, suggesting that it is "socially devastating and spiritually degrading."[6]

Architects and urban planners aren't the only ones blaming the suburban life for the current angst and isolation of the majority of American people. So are "people experts" and sociologists. Communications scientist John Locke has this to say:

> The world's longest-acting vocal suppressant has undoubtedly been urbanization. After World War II, ownership of homes increased, suburbs formed, commuting intensified, and people began to isolate themselves in homes with television sets and other private amusements. . . . In our modern, complex societies, we are suffering from a social form of progressive aphonia. That is, we are losing our personal voices. During a period in which feelings of isolation and loneliness are on the rise, too many of us are becoming emotionally and socially mute.[7]

This research, similar results of the research, and the real-life stories of the tragedy of isolation are unending. I believe it's time for church leaders to take a long, hard look at the negative effects of the suburb on the development of biblical community. The fact of the matter is, this is where most church members live. As we ponder the question of how to develop authentic Christian community, we must carefully probe the obstacle presented by the places we have created in which to live. Too often church leaders lay out biblical mandates for the church community and wonder why people are not committed to it. We must not only interpret the ancient text of Scripture, we must also interpret the contemporary culture if we hope to fulfill the goal of helping people become fully developing followers of Christ in the context of authentic community.

SOLITARY CONFINEMENT

When Bob and Karen Johnson are at home, there is no one with whom to talk or connect. There is no one walking by—not even themselves—contrary to what they were thinking and hoping would happen after they moved to their new home. Everyone seems to be connected to their homestead only through a closed-in automobile. As a matter of fact, various studies have suggested that walking has decreased significantly in America in the last twenty years. John Locke proposes that many people have traded in real walking for a virtual brand: ambulating on motorized treadmills while watching television or listening to their favorite tunes, neither reaching physical destinations nor satisfying social appetites, but "pretty much keeping to themselves."[8]

While at home the Johnsons turn to television or newspaper for local news, and now "real time" global news as well. Samaritanship is seldom covered on the news (unless, of course, a young man helps an elderly woman across the street and she falls in the process, then sues the man). Because sizzle is what sells, the newspeople tell Bob and Karen that the neighbors around them are predominantly crooks and murderers, even though only a relatively few Americans are actually severely immoral and devious. This serves only to intensify the Johnsons' fear. They install alarm systems, keep their doors locked at all times, and require their children to play in the backyard, which is surrounded by a six-foot privacy fence.

When the Johnsons go out for routine errands, they seldom encounter or relate to actual, real live people anymore. They get gas at a station where there is no attendant. Bob just sticks his credit card in the automated machine, fills up his gas tank, and takes off, not speaking to a single person in the process. Like most banking experiences these days, the Johnsons' experience is an automated one. (In some banks in America, you're now charged a three-dollar fee to talk to an actual person.) When the Johnsons venture out to the large mall fifteen minutes away, they find themselves surrounded by a multitude of people, but they know no one. People seem to work hard at avoiding conversation.

Because their experience outside the walls of their home seldom involves meaningful human interaction anyway, the Johnsons are discovering that it's more convenient to do their banking and shopping on the Internet. Yet, while it's more convenient, the reality is, it's not helping them with their boredom and loneliness.

Once a year the Johnsons venture out to the local amusement park. They even made the "great American Dream" journey out to Disneyland. At these places they are literally surrounded by thousands of people. The parks re-create little townlike structures that seek to give you the impression that everyone is kinfolk or a close family friend. Yet, there's no denying the truth: The Johnsons know no one, and they spend much of the day standing in long lines, uncomfortably close to people they know nothing about. Happily, the theme parks have provided strategically located TV monitors to enhance the waiting experience, so that people can ignore each other more comfortably.

When the Johnsons go to work, they go in opposite directions. They had never given much thought to the location of their work in relationship to their home. With high-speed freeways, initiated by President Eisenhower in the 1950s, and automobiles allowed to travel sixty-five or seventy miles per hour on these freeways, who really cares anyway? In the Johnsons' metropolitan area, the freeways have HOV (High Occupancy Vehicle) lanes for cars with more than one person in them. On those many evenings when Bob and Karen are both stuck in a freeway traffic jam on their way home, they often think just how nice it would be to hop over into an HOV lane—after all, no one else is using it.

On many evenings, the Johnsons overestimate how many errands they can run with their fast-moving metal homes on wheels, with the result that they find themselves eating fast food in the car. Bob has had so many dining experiences in the car that he has pondered buying a car equipped with a foldout dining table to go with the six cup holders already installed.

THE CHURCH—PART OF THE PRISON SYSTEM

Everything and everyone in the Johnsons' life is disconnected. Their church experience is no different. The Johnsons enjoy the sermons, but they had really hoped for a deeper sense of community. They thought they might experience community through their small group, but now, after a year, they've begun to miss on average one of the two monthly meetings because they just can't fit it into their schedule. Their hearts are in the right place, but their electronic palm-held calendars just can't work it out. While the once-a-month gathering doesn't add up to a meaningful experience for them, in reality the every-other-week thing didn't do it either. What they hoped would be the answer to their search to belong has turned out to be yet another world to manage—one that feels contrived and forced.

The Johnsons are beginning to contemplate checking out another church. They are unable to pinpoint exactly what they think is wrong with the church they're in, but in America, if you have any kind of inkling that your needs are not being met, you tend to move on. So in time the Johnsons will just slip out the door, never to return. Maybe someone will make a phone call, or they may have one encounter with a well-meaning church member about their whereabouts, but essentially their absence will go unnoticed. And their search for satisfaction continues.

8

FINDING A COMMON PLACE

There's a line from the 1993 box office hit movie *Jurassic Park* that aptly describes the American lifestyle. At one point in the movie a group of people, comprised of a lawyer and some "salt of the earth" paleontologists, are sitting around a large conference table. It finally sinks in that eccentric billionaire John Hammond has created a genetic wonder world of prehistoric dinosaurs reconstructed from the DNA of dinosaur blood extracted from ancient mosquitoes. The paleontologists are caught up in the marvel of actually seeing flesh on the bones they have been digging up for years; the lawyer sees dollar signs. Only one character, John Malcolm (played by Jeff Goldblum), offers a stern word of caution and concern. He says, "Your scientists were so preoccupied with whether or not they could, they didn't stop to think if they should!"[1]

This confrontational statement can and should be applied to the American way of life adopted over the past fifty years. When we began to build our sprawling suburbs, superhighway systems, and faster automobiles in the 1950s, we apparently only asked, "Can we do it?"—not "Should we do it?" Looking back at fifty years of suburban life, I would suggest that we could do it—because we did—but we should not have done it in the manner in which we did it. We ignored what our ancestors had learned about designing a place where people could live together and grow in community. They taught us, if only we had paid attention, that there are principles governing how to build places that promote close-knit human community. While modern-day circumstances are different, Americans have responded in much the same way the people of Israel did to the charge Jeremiah gave them over 2,500 years ago:

> This is what the LORD says:
> "Stand at the crossroads and look;
>   ask for the ancient paths,
> ask where the good way is, and walk in it,
>   and you will find rest for your souls.
>   But you said, 'We will not walk in it.'"[2]

This chapter will reveal that Bob and Karen Johnson have made some critical decisions that they obviously *could* have made but probably *should* not have made—and they are not alone.

FIVE CHARACTERISTICS OF COMMUNITY AROUND A COMMON PLACE

When we built our suburban homes and our new cities, we not only ignored what those who had gone before us could teach us about human community, we also ignored what the Bible teaches about biblical community. Biblical community is a collection of people who gather around a common biblical purpose and common principles.

However, a group of people can be committed to the Bible from its opening page to its concluding page and still not be a community. By the same token, a group of people can experience community and not be biblical in its purpose. What does this mean? That there are some common characteristics shared by groups of people who experience true community around a common place. When these five characteristics are fully functioning, they seem to facilitate the chemistry for community. When one or more is absent, something essential is lost. If all five are missing, it's highly probable that human community is not being experienced, regardless of the group's commitment to the Bible. As you read about each characteristic, evaluate whether it is present and functioning within your "community."

Spontaneity

Spontaneity is defined as "acting or taking place without any outside force or cause."[3] Places of effective community exhibit this very characteristic. While there are gatherings that are planned with rich tradition and elaborate ritual, most of the gatherings are unplanned—that is, spontaneous.

Take, for example, the small-town neighborhoods in America before the 1950s. People may have had one car per family; many simply used public transportation. If a family did own a car, it was usually driven to work by the man of the house. Throughout the course of the day the wife would need to shop for groceries or other staple items; she may even need to get to the town square's post office to check for mail. Everyone else in the neighborhood needed to do the same. In those days houses were located within walking distance of places of work and retail shops. As a result, numerous times in a single day people in the neighborhood would walk by other homes—homes cropped closely to the street, with a sidewalk in between. Oftentimes family members were found outside, sitting on the front porch and sipping iced tea. They were outside because there was no central air conditioning in the house; the porch was the place that held the most breeze for the money. There was nothing of particular interest on television—which most people didn't own anyway. They were very likely drinking simple brewed tea to keep themselves from dehydrating—not the exotic flavored teas we drink today as the "hip" thing to do. Whenever Mrs. Jones would walk by on her way to the store to get some fresh milk or eggs, the family on the porch would call out a greeting. They might even take the time to "shoot the breeze" over a glass of tea. Their interaction wasn't a planned event but a spontaneous encounter in which human contact was made and the local "gossip chain" was usually kept alive.

Consider the lives of the children in these old-fashioned neighborhoods. While Dad was at work, did little Johnny ask Mom if he could go over to Billy's house on the other side of town? Did Mom agree and pull her seven-passenger van out of the rear-entry garage and take her beloved son over to Billy's house twenty minutes away? Well, if truth be told, this wouldn't have happened! First, many families didn't even own a car, let alone a seven-passenger luxury van. Children were expected to play in the neighborhood with the children who lived there. There were relatively few organized sports. Parents were not reduced to playing the role of licensed chauffeur and entertainment specialist. Children were expected to use their imagination, on a nonexistent monetary budget, to create a day filled with spontaneous play. They never got away with a lot of mischief, because the other neighbors were out on their front porches, taking a walk to run a necessary errand, or working in their backyards—which were not, by the way, protected by six-foot privacy fences. If little Johnny was up to something, Mom and Dad would most likely know about it before he came home for supper.

This kind of spontaneous activity was not just characteristic of pre-World War II American neighborhoods; it has been the experience of 99.9 percent of human civilization before that. Only in the last fifty years have people been robbed of their spontaneity. Jesus experienced it with his disciples. They didn't have to schedule teaching times or mealtimes, because they were together already. The Old Testament patriarch Jacob didn't have to wonder whether his eldest son, Reuben, would remember to call each night; Reuben was living in the tent next door. Every night the family members would gather by the fire and tell stories and laugh together. For their entertainment they didn't travel twenty minutes away to the late-night movie theater, equipped with the latest and best high-tech features, stadium seating, and football-field-size screen. That kind of entertainment just didn't exist. When the sun went down, the lights were out. Only the light from an oil lamp or a small fire was available for family members to gather around and talk.

John Locke tells us that "our spontaneity has taken a plunge."[4] Most Americans don't know that they lost it, or that they ever had it, for that matter. But it seems that they do long for it. For most of the last decade of the twentieth century, two television shows, *Seinfeld* and *Friends,* consistently received the top awards from the People's Choice Awards, whose honorees are chosen by a special opinion poll of thousands of Americans.[5] What both shows have in common is a small group of friends who go in and out of each other's lives and apartments spontaneously more times in a half hour than most "real" Americans experience in a year. *Seinfeld* even promoted itself as a show "about nothing." Why would busy Americans watch a show about nothing? Because it wasn't about nothing—it was about a group of great friends spending a lot of spontaneous time together, talking about everyday stuff and loving every minute of it. Apparently so did the people who watched the shows.

If Americans are going to find fulfillment in their search to belong, they must find a small band of people who spontaneously go in and out of each other's lives. The small group the Johnsons had joined at church seemed to hold this promise, but the desired result was never achieved—at least in part because *this* type of small group requires everything to be planned in advance or it doesn't happen. (As a matter of fact, one of the cardinal rules for a leader of a small group is that you must plan the next meeting before the last one ends or you may never be able to coordinate schedules to get back together again.) It's not that the Johnsons and the other group members don't want spontaneous encounters, it simply isn't the way their lives work. The distance between friends, which can only be overcome through careful planning and some kind of a commute, places spontaneity out of reach. Once again we see that the characteristics of community go against the grain of our contemporary culture, that is, they are countercultural. Yet, this shouldn't surprise us. The "me" world we've created for ourselves is not a compatible environment for the principles that govern human community.

Availability

Closely akin to spontaneity is the characteristic of *availability*. Those who have found a meaningful experience of life together discover that most of the time it is because their comrades are ready, willing, and eager to lend an ear or a hand—or even to offer the simple gift of their presence. It's not that these people do not have important things to do; it's just that they see being available to each other as more important than most of the things we in today's society deem important—the things that keep us continually on the road to nowhere.

In other times and in other cultures a *screen* was commonly understood as a lightweight meshed-wire door designed to let fresh air in the house, keep bugs out, and signal to the neighbors that someone was home. It was a sort of invitation. In our suburban way of life, a screen has come to carry the opposite connotation. It does not filter out bugs, but people. Peepholes, Caller ID, answering machines, and voice mailboxes give us the option to say yes to one and no to another. Mind you, this is not all bad. The technological world we have created for ourselves enables the entire world to be a potential caller. Most of the calls we receive are from strangers trying to sell us something—in the end, preying on our loneliness. At the same time, most of us really do long for a true friend to drop by or call—but we understand when they don't; after all, everybody really is so very busy.

In the past, if a person who lived in a place of true community wanted to chat with a friend, the chances were good that the friend would be instantly available because they both lived within walking distance of one another—you see, for the most part, they didn't have the kind of mobility options we have today. The person was available because there really were no other places to be.

We have already voiced the opinion that most of us don't know the people who live around us. So, instead of *getting* to know these people, we typically opt to engage in contractual friendships with those who are most like us or with those we like the best, regardless of where they live. Why? Because this is one thing we *can* do. The unspoken goal of contractual friendship is to "associate up"—usually as it relates to economic class.

There are significant problems in adopting this style of contrived community. First and foremost, it isn't pleasing to God. Jesus scolded the religious leaders of his day for trying to define one's neighbor in any sort of restricted way. One expert of the law tried to justify himself as a good neighbor but wanted his evaluation to include only those of his own race and status. In response, Jesus told the famous story of the Good Samaritan, thereby dismantling this faulty view of community.[6]

In an article in the *Cornell Law Review*, Greg Alexander challenges this breed of friendships as well. Alexander views the tensions around community in American life as a conflict between the *contractarian* and *communitarian* theories of community. The former, related to a rational-choice theory, views individuals as atomistic, not connected to each other except as they agree to be connected for personal benefit. In the communitarian ideal, "individuals are embedded in society, connected not only through their common humanity but through the social structures they jointly create and benefit from."[7]

The second significant problem with contractual friendships is this: They don't really work. As time and practice have proved, we are not really available for each other apart from precise planning. We might take a moment to look out our kitchen window to see if someone is available, but it isn't likely that we would drive across town on the hunch that a friend will be home and free to talk with you. This isn't to say, of course, that the intentions are not good. It is simply to say—*it doesn't really work*. Imagine a monk not being happy with the type of people who reside in his monastery. So he opts to develop his deepest friendships with guys in the monastery thirty miles away. Ludicrous, you say. It would never happen. You see, monks may lack mobility, but they do maintain the highest level of availability. This is one of the reasons their experience of community is such a positive one. If we hired a Benedictine monk to guide us toward a more simple way of life, I'm convinced he would tell us that we can't get where we want to go given the lifestyle we have chosen. He would recommend a "radical reinventing" that includes freeing up more time to be available for community. The question is, how badly do we want community?

Frequency

Another characteristic of community that promotes the value of a common place is *frequency*. Simply put, people who are satisfied with the experience of community are those who spend a great deal of time together. In the book of Acts we are given a rare peek into the wonderful and effective community of the "First Church of Jerusalem":

> *They devoted themselves to the apostles' teaching and to the fellowship, to the breaking of bread and to prayer.[8]*

Luke tells us that this close-knit group of Christ-followers devoted themselves to four principal things: the apostles' teaching, fellowship, the breaking of bread, and prayer. Beginning in verse 43 of Acts 2, and continuing on for several verses, we are shown the outcome of their community devotion. Miracles took place, people's lives were being changed, the believers cared deeply and sacrificially for each other, new people were coming to know Christ—and as a result their group grew rapidly. The Bible says they even enjoyed a spectacular reputation in the surrounding community. But there is one aspect of their fellowship most modern-day believers overlook—how often they got together: "Every day they continued to meet together."[9]

The big issue in Bob and Karen's church is how often should a small group meet—once a week, or every other week. What we are learning from studying healthy places of community is that neither once a week nor every other week is enough to create the results of real community. If we want the outcome of the "First Church of Jerusalem," we must be willing to put in the same level of commitment. It doesn't make sense to input one-seventh or one-fourteenth of all the available time and expect 100 percent of the results.

You are no doubt shaking your head in disbelief at such a suggestion. But this kind of daily interaction has been a dominant characteristic and requirement of community throughout history. In India a small group of Christians in a village gather every day to pray. You can see the depth of their love for each other as you view the videotape of their meeting—it's that evident. Christians in India need our financial resources to help them accomplish Christ's mission, but they *don't* need our style of church. The worst thing we could do is to "colonialize" the American church model in India, imposing it on them. Rather, we should rejoice to give them all our money to teach us how they do Christian community.

Even in the college fraternity house, the notion of multiple encounters in a given day with the same people is not seen as unusual but the norm. (Maybe this explains why so many people have such fond memories of their college days.) Add as an overlay a common commitment to Christ, like Campus Crusade for Christ does, and it thoroughly ruins the graduate's chances of a happy assimilation into today's "individualized" church.

The American lifestyle does not represent the norm in the world today but the exception. The world we've created for ourselves pulls us apart from daily interaction, making us the loneliest people in the world.

This social condition has progressively worsened in the last fifty years, much like the frog placed in a pot of room-temperature water. When the temperature was slowly turned up, little by little, he was unaware of what was happening—he, like us, being boiled to death and never realizing it. John Locke lays bare a very telling study of American life:

> Each year in a large and respected poll, the General Social Survey, Americans from a range of demographic groups are asked how often they spend an evening socializing with a neighbor. In 1974 nearly one in four Americans visited with a neighbor several times a week. By 1994, that figure had declined to 16 percent. But in 1994 there was a shocking increase in the number of people who had *never* spent an evening with a neighbor—from one in five to nearly one in three—a 41 percent increase since the same question was asked twenty years earlier.[10]

The isolated places in which we live have given rise to an unprecedented number of practicing counselors in the marketplace. I would never want to imply that mental health professionals are not needed to help us through some of the struggles we encounter in life. However, people often employ them as nothing more than a "paid friend." In my opinion, I would cautiously suggest that roughly 80 percent of this industry has been created in the last twenty-five years as an alternative to what true community used to provide free of charge. I see churches struggle as they try to create community, as they try to establish strong, properly functioning small groups, in a "place," or lack of place, where friendships are outsourced to paid professionals. As they strategize to create community today, church leaders must find a way to address these issues. Jim Petersen lays it out in the simplest of chromatic terms: "Body Life is 24 hours a day, 7 days a week, and embraces the full spectrum of our activities."[11] If people are not willing to restructure their lives and their time to get to the heart of this characteristic of frequency—and trust me, it can be done—the experience of true community will continue to elude them. Unless we make these changes, we will never have the kind of community the "First Church of Jerusalem" had, and we should stop pretending that we do.

Common Meals

It is hard to believe that something as mundane as sharing a meal together could be included in the list of the top characteristics of community, but it is. Now, note carefully, it's not just eating, but eating *together*. In a story about Dr. Daniel Sack, author of *Whitebread Protestants: Food and Religion in American Culture*, writer Jeffrey Weiss from *The Dallas Morning News* begins his article with these words: "The casseroles and Jell-O molds of the traditional Protestant potluck supper may seem unlikely sources for serious insight. But Daniel Sack, associate director for the Material History of American Religion project, says there is important information about belief and custom hidden among the beanie-weenies."[12]

Although many Bible readers tend to overlook it, eating together was a significant part of the early church experience: "Every day they continued to meet together. . . . They broke bread in their homes and ate together with glad and sincere hearts."[13] There is something vitally important and special about sharing a meal together. Just consider the fact that the Lord's Supper (an act of partaking together of food and drink) is one of the few New Testament rituals we are commanded to observe. Eberhard Arnold, who founded the Bruderhof Communities, put it eloquently when he wrote, "Symbolism can be found in the trivialities of existence, too: when approached with reverence, even daily rites such as mealtime can become consecrated festivals of community."[14]

By and large the concept of eating together has become foreign to the American culture. It is rare for the average American family to share two to three meals together during the week. Look more closely at the Johnson family, and you will see that the children's sports activities and a lot of extra hours at the office account for most of the meals missed together at night. Just try once to suggest that a small group of people share a meal a couple of times a week, and see how many people will laugh at you because they can't even manage to do that with their own families. Admittedly, given our current lifestyles, this *is* an unreasonable expectation—which is precisely why making progress toward real community will take major restructuring. When we fail to practice the community value of eating together, something serious is lost in the quality of our contemporary experience of community.

Geography

The characteristic of community that facilitates and drives the previous four is *geography*. The simple fact is that in all places of effective community people live in close proximity to each other—and the closer the better! Consider Jesus and his disciples. To those he encountered, Jesus extended the invitation, "Come, follow me," not "Come, make the commute each day." The late Henri Nouwen left a prestigious Ivy League professorship to become the executive director of L'Arche, a residential community for mentally and physically challenged people. He did so because of what he perceived as a divine call. What he found at L'Arche was the richest community he had ever experienced. However, soon after he arrived he fell apart. In his own words he tells the story:

> After many years of life in universities, where I never felt fully at home, I had become a member of L'Arche, a community of men and women with disabilities. I had been received with open arms, given all the attention and affection I could hope for, and offered a safe and loving place to grow spiritually as well as emotionally. Everything seemed ideal. But precisely at that time I fell apart—as if I needed a safe place to hit bottom.[15]

Christian psychologist Larry Crabb offers this insightful commentary regarding Nouwen's experience:

> When he gave them [his prestigious career and all it offered him] up for life with people who were not impressed by such things, perhaps his repressed desire to be loved rather than merely admired overwhelmed him.

The taste of love that his new community provided may have awakened deeper longings than he ever knew existed, longings that he feared would never be satisfied.[16]

We learn from Henri Nouwen's experience that community does not necessarily require profound intelligence, but it does require being geographically close enough to be available for each other spontaneously and frequently enough to feel safe and loved.

One lady wrote of her experience in a residential community with a group of women who lived together in one house. While not everything about it was positive, on the whole it was remarkably meaningful for her. Soon after getting married she abandoned this style of relationships. She began to attend her husband's church-sponsored small group. Here's her honest assessment of that experience: "Living in residential community raised my standards. For several months I attended my husband's church small group. I thought, 'This is intimacy? This is challenge?' After years of prayer, fellowship, and everyday life with five close roommates, a weekly meeting with a dozen people seemed shallow."[17]

The Johnsons' suburban small group experience is not a bad thing; it's just not enough. For their experience to go to the next level of meaning, it should be "pedestrian accessible"; you should be able to walk to get to each other. In the Western world, as it comes to expression in the suburb where the Johnsons live, this means finding community in a neighborhood. You can contract with a collection of the brightest, smartest, strongest, prettiest, and most spiritual people to form a small group, but if they are not in close proximity (that is, living within walking distance), it just won't compare to what poor people in a House of Prayer in India experience. Their village closeness and their commitment to Christ and to each other daily make their life together a sight to behold. Once you see it, you will emphatically want it for yourself.

Of course, many would raise objections to this countercultural concept of geographic-based relationships. With Internet chat rooms we *can* have instant friendships with anyone at any time and anywhere in the world for a minimal cost. Critics would also add that nowhere in America are social networks established today according to geography— and they would be right. However, this is not a strong argument to abandon the rediscovery of neighborhood, especially when you consider that the current model has produced what many social experts call "the loneliest people on the face of the earth." I also understand that there are negative reactions that are more personal in nature. Because we naturally want to defend the quality of the relationships we have already formed, many of us will be offended by this exposé on the potential weaknesses of nongeographic friendships. All I would plead for as you respond to my subjective and personal evaluation is an open mind.

Having said all this, I hasten to add that geographic-based community has its share of problems and challenges. Just ponder for a moment the small, old-fashioned town with a main street where everyone works and shops, a town where houses are all pretty much within walking distance. Some who live there would say that they do not experience intimacy but an invasion of their privacy! Everybody knows everything about you and might even, on occasion, use their knowledge to feed the local gossip mill. This isn't true community; rather, it can be classified as "community without character." The good news is, this can be changed. By contrast, most people who live in suburban America are left alone, and news about their life is kept secret (at least in part because people don't care). Real community is simply not accessible to them. In the former situation, it's a matter of changing the ethics of community; in the latter, it's a matter of trying to find community at all.

Take a man and a woman with three children and stick them together under one roof, and you'll get moments of intense conflict and irritation. But most people are not willing to forsake family life just because it has its challenging moments. They stick with it not because it is easy but because it is meaningful. So it is with Christian community as well. If everybody is spread out geographically so that they see each other just once a week or once a month, it might be less burdensome from a scheduling perspective, but it will most likely not be meaningful. One of the biggest challenges in the effort to build community is to convince people to choose something that may not necessarily be easy, but is nonetheless good for them.

The profundity of this characteristic of geography lies in the simple accessibility it offers people. If Bob and Karen were to find their most significant relationships within their neighborhood, these relationships would begin to meet some of their deepest needs. But because the Johnsons are a product of their culture, they just can't see how this could work. A lot of people don't know *anyone* in their neighborhood, let alone

9

REDISCOVERING NEIGHBORHOOD

As Bob and Karen are introduced to the idea of simplifying the many disconnected worlds they manage into one hub, to be built around Christian relationships within a neighborhood, they breathe a sigh of relief. Yet, they can't see how it could work. Well, it can and does work for many people. The Johnsons need to remember that what currently defines their lifestyle and time commitments is not working. While this commitment to community will take time and experimentation, something new must be attempted. If we continue using the same methods, we should not expect to achieve different results. Princeton professor Robert Wuthnow cites this testimony, which emerged out of his research on America's quest for community:

> I used to be in this group of people who met weekly, and that was a specific circle of friends where we really did help each other out, sharing problems, sharing whatever. Now my friends are more linear. I'm friends with this person and I'm friends with that person, but I don't have a circle of friends who sort of know each other right now.[1]

Wuthnow's comments on this testimony form a crucial foundation for establishing why the Johnsons must seek a new paradigm for living.

> The difference is that a circle provides for more internal accountability than a series of linear relationships. If your friends don't know each other, you (even without thinking about it) play up one side of yourself to this friend and a different side to someone else. One friend, for example, can be a confidant on spiritual issues; another can share babysitting but have no spiritual points of intersection at all. When your friends all know each other because they are in the same group, you are more likely to experience the tendency toward personal consistency that fellow believers refer to as *discipleship.* Your friends can compare notes to see if you are treating them all the same. They can decide whether you need advice. For them to all get along with each other, they are likely to agree on certain principles themselves. And this agreement will minimize your chances of being pulled in widely different directions.[2]

Bob and Karen long to have a circle of friends with whom they can mutually share their dreams and fears. A series of disconnected linear relationships will never achieve this; it takes a cohesive circle of friends. If the Johnsons are serious about achieving their private goal, they must exchange their current linear strategy for a circular one. While some will argue that there are many ways to accomplish this goal of intimate community, experience and history have proven that people who share a common place are in the best position to achieve this. The best way to describe it in familiar language is to suggest that the

Johnsons must rediscover the ancient concept of *neighborhood*. It's an idea that goes beyond the small group meeting—it is truly, in the words of Dietrich Bonhoeffer, "life together." Nothing else will come close.

THE BEGINNINGS OF A CULTURAL SHIFT

While critics of this concept say it's already been tried and claim that social networks are not and will not be established by geography, there is solid evidence to show that American culture is moving in this direction. The December 8, 1997, issue of *Time* magazine devoted the lead story to this social shift:

> A new kind of "white flight" is going on in America today, but unlike the middle-class exodus from multi-ethnic cities to the suburbs a generation ago, this middle-class migration is from crowded, predominantly white suburbs to small towns and rural counties. Rural America has enjoyed a new inflow of 2 million people this decade—that is, 2 million more people have moved from metropolitan centers to rural areas than have gone the traditional small-town-to-big-city route. (In the 1980s, by contrast, rural areas suffered a net loss of 1.4 million people.) Thanks to the newcomers, 75% of the nation's rural counties are growing again after years of decline....
> Inevitably, a cottage industry is springing up to service the newcomers. At least four recent books promise to teach cityfolk how to find the village of their dreams, and one entrepreneur has a company, the Greener Pastures Institutes, that helps urbanites engineer the great escape....Whether young or old, the new émigrés share a sense that they're reinventing their lives in places that seem purer than the suburban moonscape one émigré

calls "the United States of Generica." ... These new émi-
grés are acting out a fantasy shared by tens of millions of
Americans.[3]

Americans are on the run in search of smaller and more
intimate places in which to live and grow. Many might
argue that these people don't know what they're doing and
can't expect immediate community bliss by barging in on
a small-town party. Certainly it's true you can't expect to
experience intimate community immediately; however,
these activities do show that a shift is taking place.
Americans *are* taking a more active role in their search to
belong.

A Radical Reinventing

It is not reasonable to expect that everyone will move
from the suburbs to a smaller town. So, given the scenario
of staying in their suburban home, how might a family like
the Johnsons begin to create community? Because of the
architectural forces that mitigate against achieving community in the suburb, its pursuit will have to be intentional.
It will require making difficult changes and learning the art
of saying no to all the things we *can* do in our fully functional metropolises. It will be a process that struggles to
coexist with the transitioning of lifestyle paradigms. If you
venture on this journey, you will be pioneering an ancient
idea for a new day—and pioneers are always criticized and
misunderstood. If you have the determination and stamina
to stay with the adventure and follow the governing principles as purely as you know how, you will one day begin
to realize dividends from your investment. It could take six
months, or it could take two years or more.

Let me share several specific tips for engineering your "great escape." (By the way, if you have a tough time seeing how this vision can be accomplished in your current neighborhood, read these steps as though you were going to move to a new place and make a fresh start. One of the biggest mistakes people make today is looking only to buy a house, not to find a neighborhood. We spend a lot of money for an inspection to ensure the quality of the home's construction, yet because relationships are more important than sticks and bricks, common sense suggests that it would be wise to conduct a neighborhood inspection as well.)

Cut Down the Commute

If at all possible, live in the neighborhood closest to your workplace. If it isn't possible, try to rearrange your schedule to avoid traffic jams. If you're spending two or three hours a day commuting, it's difficult to have much time left for anything else.

Live Off a Single Income

If you have children at home, it makes the most sense to have one person at home full-time to manage meals and oversee the children's homework so they get it done early enough to leave time open in the evening. For those who begin these tasks after work hours, it eats into those precious hours for daily community sharing with others. For most suburban families where both the mother and father work and commute long distances, it is virtually impossible for them to have meals together as a family, let alone to eat meals with their neighbors. (Incidentally, for the single parent, how beneficial it would be if at least a few meals a week could be shared with neighbors in order to lighten his or her load.)

If this solution is not within your grasp, here are two options to consider: First, take advantage of today's technology and pursue work that can be done at home with flexible work hours. The second idea is simple but radical. Look for a home that can be funded on less money—preferably on one income. The irony of American family economics today is that we purchase big and beautiful homes that take two incomes to sustain, and yet we hardly spend any time in them.

Choose Stability

Most families move every two to five years. The most common reason is a company transfer or a new job. Now, it is certainly true that on occasion work will dry up in a town or city, with the result that one is forced to move on to provide the basic necessities for the family. However, the reality is, more often than not, people are merely chasing an extra $5,000–$10,000 a year.

The difficulty with this mind-set is that it never gives a chance for relational roots to grow deep enough to matter. Most pastors have come to realize that they can plan for new members to be a part of the church for only two to five years before these members move again. So prevalent is this mobility phenomenon that most people assume a new relationship isn't going to last long before one or the other of them (or both) moves away—so why bother getting started in the first place, the thinking goes. While sometimes we *must* move or are responding to a valid conviction to relocate to another place, we need to value stability and longevity—characteristics that give community a real chance.

Set Geographic Boundaries

Individual homes are the only real defined space in the suburb. Therefore, one of the easiest steps of creating community in a suburb is to create your own geographic boundaries. Scope out a one-mile radius around your home. This is your place of concentration. For most suburban areas this will include anywhere from one hundred to two hundred homes. Seek to do as much within this radius as possible. Shop in this zone; send your children to schools there. Most important, concentrate the development of your Christian community within this circle.

Identify a Core

Bring the matter to God in prayer, and then seek out one or two Christian families within your neighborhood that would agree to establish this kind of community. While it isn't absolutely essential that these families attend the same church, it is preferable. Worshiping together at the same place on Sunday and being connected to the same body of Christians give you that much more in common.

Free Up Your Schedule

Over the next six months, begin to free up your calendar. Make a master list of the things you do, and begin to say no to those things that splinter your life and leave you feeling hurried and stressed. This will mean you will say no to some of the things you enjoy—and that will be hard. It will involve eliminating some—not all—of your children's sports commitments and other activities—and that will be hard also. It will entail backing out of some of your own commitments—even church commitments, such as serving on committees; the truth is, these "good" commitments can pull you away from an experience of deep community as effectively as can secular events. As you begin making these changes, if others ask why you're no longer involved in these activities, tell them you are trying to simplify your life. Most will appreciate your effort. However, be careful not to preach to others or try to force them to do the same. A significant number of people won't get it or won't want it for themselves, and you are almost guaranteed to offend them in some way or another.

Spend Time Together

Begin spending time together with the one to two families you have sought out within your neighborhood. Begin with sharing a dinner together where everyone brings something—the combined effort should prevent anyone from feeling too stressed. If it doesn't, keep adjusting your arrangements until it does. If you can't do dinner, do dessert. Take walks together in the neighborhood. (A word of caution: At first your neighbors may call the police to check out these "strangers" making their way through the neighborhood without biker shorts and a Walkman!) Rent a classic movie, and watch it together on a Friday night. If three families share the cost, it will add up to thirty-three cents a family. The list of possibilities is unlimited. And the beauty of it is, community doesn't have to cost a lot of money.

Agree to a Common Purpose

A common place is the best facilitator of community, but it does not guarantee community; to achieve community requires a *common purpose.* For a community to be biblical the common purpose must be biblical. Talk to your church leaders about the purposes they would like to see you embrace; by doing so, it enables you to be connected to the broader body of Christ in your community. Look back over chapters 4 and 5 for additional assistance in establishing this vital component. It may be a good idea for the members of the group to agree to a written covenant that spells out their common purpose (see, for example, the covenant found on pages 82–83).

Play in the Front Yard Together

Most suburban homes today are built with porches as facades. They give the *appearance* of a place where people hang out to talk and laugh, but seldom, if ever, is anyone found there. One of the simplest and most practical things you can do to create community in your neighborhood is to play in the front yard. While many suburban neighborhoods don't have sidewalks because of a lack of meaningful places to walk—and the streets are designed to serve cars, not people—it is still possible to rediscover the front of the house, and even the streets of neighborhoods, as the new hangout for the family. Purchase some lawn chairs or a swing, and sit in the front yard in the evenings and on weekends. Bring out a jug of iced tea with some extra glasses. It may take awhile for others to catch on, but be patient. Play kickball in the streets. A neighbor might on occasion complain that the ball landed in their petunias, but eventually they'll join in the festivities. Wave to people driving by in their cars; one day they'll stop by. Have the other Christian families in your neighborhood stop by for a visit. Invite children in the neighborhood to join in whatever game or activity that happens to be going on. A cul-de-sac makes for one of the best layouts for these activities, but it is not essential in order to enjoy an experience of community in the front yard.

Orient Yourselves to the Rules of Being a Good Neighbor

Make it a goal to find favor with your neighbors because of the kindness and character of your life.[4] Here are a handful of guiding principles:

- Take care of your property; if you don't do it for yourself, at least do it for your neighbors.
- Stop by and see neighbors spontaneously. However, if the visit is unplanned, agree to stay no more than ten minutes. People who have not yet restructured their lives will love the visit but most likely won't have time for it. If you stop by and see a neighbor working on a project, don't allow them to stop working—even if they say it's okay. The best thing to do is pitch in and help.
- If your dog barks all the time, come up with a solution.

- Borrow stuff from your neighbors; it gives you a great excuse to see them. However, make sure when you return it that it's cleaner than when you borrowed it. If you break it, replace it with something comparable.
- Use common sense.
- Here is a novel idea: "Do to others what you would have them do to you."[5]

Find a Purpose to Bring All the Neighbors Together

Find something the neighbors can rally around as a way to make the neighborhood a better place to live. Petition to get a stop sign installed. Organize a Neighborhood Block Watch. Have an old-fashioned block party. Designate each Wednesday "volleyball night" or "basketball night." All these activities take abundant amounts of interaction to pull off—just the thing you need in order to form the foundation for community.

Rediscover the Lord's Day

If you are a Christian, a spiritual core is at the center of your desire for community. This spiritual core is what centers our relationships on the person of Jesus Christ. In order to focus on this key unifying quality, we would do well to set aside the Lord's Day, or Sunday.[6] For us in our church it begins with corporate worship at the church building and ends with a gathering of a handful of families in our neighborhood—the Home Group. While the Home Group does not, by any means, exhaust the spiritual objective, it finds its primary expression here. For suburban Americans there is probably no better time to accomplish this than on a Sunday. While an increasing number of activities are finding their way to Sunday, it is still the day many workplaces respect as a day off. Therefore, most American Christians have the opportunity to reclaim the ancient and worthwhile concept of "the Lord's Day." It means that the day can be free of work, either at the office or at the home; it means that you can guide your family to focus on worship and rest. As other activities begin to compete for this time slot, you simply say no. Here is one model for how the day may be structured:

Attend worship at your church.

Grab a light lunch, which you have prepared the night before.

Take a refreshing nap.

Gather with the members of your Home Group (people located within your neighborhood) to enjoy dinner together and to focus on the biblical purposes and functions expressed in your covenant. The meeting should run for about three hours (from 4:00–7:00 P.M., or from 5:00–8:00 P.M.). Be conscientious about ending the gathering on time so that everyone can get home and prepare for the next day and get a good night's sleep.

Take a group of people who live in such close proximity to one another that the community characteristics—spontaneity, availability, frequency, eating together, and geography—are completely feasible, then add a solid biblical purpose (that is, the common creed, traditions, and standards mentioned in chapter 5), and you have the makings of the kind of community Jesus and the apostles envisioned for the body of Christ. In the next chapter I'll give more details about how you might structure the Home Group time together. Right now you will simply want to ask yourself, "Is this kind of community something I'm interested in trying?"

TRUE STORIES FROM THOSE WHO ARE DOING IT

There are increasing numbers of people who are reinventing their lives while continuing to live in the suburbs. They are finding the common purposes centered in Christ and lived out in a common place to be a richer experience than they ever dreamed possible. As you read their testimonies, you will see that these are people who truly belong to Christ and to each other:

> Several years ago my husband and I built a home in a neighborhood of about a hundred homes. It was a great neighborhood—perfect for raising children. Just on our street alone there must have been twelve children. All of the kids would play out front and make up games. People were always out walking and would stop to talk. We had lived in this neighborhood for about two and a half years when we came across this beautiful piece of property on one and a half acres, with lots of trees and a creek at the back of the property. We were so excited. This would be the perfect place to build our dream house and raise our four

boys. So we bought the property. We put our current house up for sale. We started with what would be the backyard—our park. We built a go-cart track, a trampoline pit, and zip lines from tree to tree. Then we built retaining walls and sidewalks and had plans drawn for the pool. The house we designed was approximately seven thousand square feet—from marble floors to granite countertops to special paint finishes. It was awesome. Finally, there it was. The American Dream! A large house and lots of property. This house had it all—except my old neighborhood. We had everything we thought we could want, but I wanted so badly to be back in my old neighborhood.

What we did not realize is that it's not the value or the size that makes a house a home; it's the neighborhood. We sold our big, beautiful "American Dream" house one year later, only to move back to "our" neighborhood in a house less than half the size. A neighborhood Home Group was forming shortly after we moved back. We meet with several neighbors each week to support each other, share faith, and try to make a difference in our community. The group grew so large so quickly that we had to split into two groups. I love my neighbors and my Home Group.

Testimony of a husband and wife
with four elementary-age boys

We both grew up in families that attended church every Sunday and assumed this meant we were Christians. It was not until we became adults that we knew differently. Surrounding yourself with Christians in a Home Group has definitely been for us a spiritual awakening. Since joining a Home Group we have become closer to Christ, our family, and our neighbors. We never have a shortage of people who will take our kids in a pinch, walk our dog, or even wash our dishes when we've had a big dinner. We have a special bond with these neighbors. Our daughters have the advantage of actually growing up in a totally committed Christian home. Our twelve-year-old daughter accepted Christ in the summer of 1999 and our eight-year-old daughter is full of questions about Christ and what that means in her life. Just recently, our youngest daughter asked me to pray with her as she was getting out of the car when I was dropping her off at school. She had remembered what we spoke about the night before at our Home Group about accepting Jesus Christ into your life and wanted to make sure she would be walking with God that day at school. She already knows that Christ is a big part of her future and is very excited about it.

Since becoming Christians and joining our church in January of 1999, we have tried to become more of a messenger for Christ. Sharing the message of Jesus Christ with our neighbors can sometimes be a difficult subject. Then there are other times—as is the case of one couple who lives across the street from us—when we speak often about how the church and knowing Jesus Christ has affected us. Quite often when we are together with them we discuss our Home Group and tell them how interesting and meaningful it is in our lives. We soon found that they were asking more and more questions about our Home Group and our church. We were at their home one night to watch a football game and met some of their old friends from college. When we were being introduced, one woman immediately said to us, "You're the couple who is getting my friends back to church." What a great feeling it was to know that not only were we spreading the word of Jesus to them, but they also were now speaking to others about it. One Sunday morning in church, it was fantastic to see them sitting in the pew with us. This couple also has grown children, and when they visit, it's always a joy to see them together, attending church. We witnessed the Holy Spirit working through the Home Group and Pantego Bible Church, as on January 23, 2000, the wife accepted Jesus Christ as her Lord and Savior. The husband is close to making this decision too. Our neighborhood Home Group will be there day by day to nurture them to maturity in Christ.

Testimony of a husband and wife
with two elementary-age girls

When my wife and I got married, neither one of us was going to church. We didn't even know the other was a Christian. We had strayed from our faith. After twelve years we started going to a church just on Sunday mornings, without any real involvement. It was a good experience, but not very motivating spiritually. And then eighteen months ago we moved into a new neighborhood and at the same time tried out a new church. We didn't dream these two events would collide so dramatically to wake us up to our relationship with Christ. A neighborhood Home Group was forming at that time, and we decided to go see what it was all about, if for no other reason than to meet some of our new neighbors. The church and the Home Group opened up an incredible path to growth and enrichment. I feel now that I didn't know before what it was to live a Christian life. We have discovered true Christian community.

True Christian community is the hardest and easiest thing that I have ever had to describe. The key is personal experience. It is like being married to the perfect mate for fifteen years: Your mate seems to know what you are thinking even before you say it. A simple look between the two of you can convey a tremendous amount of information that would be completely lost on anyone else. That is how it goes when I discuss our Christian community with other members of our Home Group. They get it. People on the outside, even some of our church friends, think we simply have a close set of friends we happen to see often. It is difficult for them to see the difference between their friendships and our community. They don't get it.

We see each other in our community three to five or more times per week. We eat together. Our kids play together. We vacation together. We enjoy sports, we entertain, and we talk. Our Christianity is at the center of our relationships, and we have developed a real trust among ourselves. We share our faith, our growth, our successes, and our struggles. Our community is not jammed into two hours of church on Sundays. In fact, our most meaningful time together occurs outside of church. It works well because it is based on spiritual faith and neighborhood convenience. It is spontaneous. You cannot be spontaneous if you have to orchestrate a visit across town with a close friend. It takes too much investment in time and effort. Instead we just cross the street or walk down the block and join in the community of our neighbors.

We have grown tremendously in the last eighteen months. Our Home Group has grown also. We have since split into four smaller Home Groups and keep growing. Our Home Group seems to act as a magnet for others in our neighborhood who are trying to find what we have. I now lead one of the new groups with my wife's help and guidance. Two years ago I would not have believed it possible. Today I would not want to live without it.

Through God's grace and the intentional nature of our church, we have discovered a tremendous gift—the gift of true community.

Testimony of a husband and wife
with a girl in college and an elementary-age boy

Finally, listen to the unfolding story of a husband and wife in their mid-fifties who have been deeply touched by the love that a close-knit neighborhood of Christ-followers demonstrates. The husband is openly considering trusting Christ with his life; the wife recently made that decision.

Husband:

> Throughout my entire life I've had a casual attitude about attending church. However, I have led what I would consider a moral life. Recently, my neighbors invited me to attend their church and their Home Group, which meets in the neighborhood. What I realized is I've only been going through the motions of being a Christian—there is more to it! Home Group consists of people extending their families into the community to talk, study, play, and portray their Christianity to all. They seem to have found a special peace. Home Group has welcomed me unconditionally and has been a constant encouragement through discussion and providing resource material to help in my search. Their support in my efforts to become a true Christian has been amazing.

Wife:

> Home Group and the church have been very stimulating to my Christianity. I have never been exposed to so many people who exude their faith in God. It's contagious!

This kind of winsome, invasive Christian community is similar to the experience of the first-century Christians—an experience described by Yale professor Wayne Meeks:

The Pauline Group's strong and intimate sense of belonging, their special beliefs and norms, their perception of their own discreteness from "the world" did not lead them to withdraw into the desert, like the Essenes of Qumran. They remained in the cities and their members continued to go about their ordinary lives in the streets and neighborhoods, shops and agora. Paul and the other leaders did not merely permit this continued interaction as something inevitable; in several instances they positively encouraged it (1 Corinthians 5:9–13).[7]

The goal of this chapter is not to encourage people to move from the suburbs to small towns; it is to show people who are trapped in the isolated cycle of linear friendships that they are not alone and that many people are doing radical and even desperate things to change their situation. I want to encourage church leaders to take advantage of this shift in its early stages. Will individual Christians and the church catch the early wave of this wonderful opportunity, or will we once again wait until we are *forced* to adopt it, losing the chance to shape the values and structures that govern it?

The postmodern world is sick of the philosophy of "being an individual at all costs," and people everywhere are searching for answers. Let the ultimate "we" organization show them the way. Well-known church consultant Lyle Schaller suggests that many people, confronted with the facts of where we are and where we might go, will either "(a) engage in denial or (b) refute most of the points of discontinuity and the probable consequences."[8] Bob and Karen Johnson have a rare opportunity to adopt a "new" way of life that is as old as human existence. The question must be asked: How badly do they want it?

10

IMPLEMENTING A COMMON PLACE

David Wells, professor of historical and systematic theology at Gordon-Conwell Theological Seminary, has written these piercing words about contemporary society: "While earlier generations of Americans were permanent residents attached to a place, we are nomads, perpetual immigrants condemned to move from place to place in our own country."[1]

While this is a statement of fact, an apt description of the place we have created for ourselves, as church leaders we cannot meekly accept it as the way things must be if we hope to introduce the twenty-first century to the power and presence of authentic biblical community. We can no longer fashion church programming on the backs of individualism, isolationism, and consumerism. We must declare this to be unacceptable, and then commit ourselves to work feverishly to provide a communal alternative. To do this we must not only look to the Bible to provide guidance, but we must also address the societal issues that got us into this mess. We need to provide bold Christian leadership in order to find the way to the higher place where we can live life the way God intended us to live from the very beginning—connected together in community.

My premise in part 2 is that one must identify an effective *common place* if they ever hope to accomplish a worthwhile and inspiring *common purpose*. A common place is the container in which a common purpose resides. A common purpose outside of community is not really a *common* purpose but merely the ideals of individuals. In *Country of Exiles: The Destruction of Place in American Life*, William Leach discusses in detail the "weakening of place as the centering presence in the lives of ordinary people."[2] I have attempted to lay out an argument—derived from the Bible, history, and dozens of scholarly research findings on current societal conditions—that the rediscovery of *neighborhood* is the essential application to discovering a common place. It is really the only option. Why? Because it is the only way we can attain the characteristics that produce authentic community, such as spontaneity, availability, and frequency. Other options are "good" ones, and they are marked by correct intentions, but at the end of the day the composite time invested in each other's lives usually falls short of what is required to build true community. It could be compared to putting ten gallons of high-performance fuel in your car for a trip that will require twenty in order to get there. The gas tank may be filled with quality gasoline, but in the end there isn't enough to get you to your desired destination. Many Christian small groups are running on fumes; others have simply run out of gas and are stranded on the side of the road, wondering what to do next.

There are several ways for pastoral leadership to reengineer their church to create a common place for community. I'd like to share the way we have chosen to design our ministry at Pantego Bible Church in order to accomplish this operating principle for community.

DEFINING PLACE

The first step is to define what a neighborhood is—a difficult task in suburban America, because the individual home is the only *functional* boundary of place. In other words, the only place today where one might functionally get enough time with another live human being in order to make a difference is in an individual household. Harvard public policy professor Robert Putnam has recently published extensive research that shows that Americans entertained friends at home 45 percent less often in the late 1990s than they did in the mid- to late-'70s. He also uncovered the rather shocking fact that between 1974 and 1998, the frequency with which Americans spent "a social evening with someone who lives in your neighborhood" fell by about one-third.[3] The home has become a place of solitary confinement. However, even this characteristic is nearly lost, as the home has become for many simply a boardinghouse where people occasionally eat and mostly just sleep. Suburbs are not only bedroom communities, but so are the houses we have purchased in our pursuit of "the better life."

Suburban neighborhoods have at least one redeeming quality, however—you can usually define the intended boundaries for a neighborhood. It can contain as few as ten houses, if it is a single street that dead-ends into a cul-de-sac, or as many as one hundred homes. *Neighborhood* can be defined as "a collection of houses that people can easily get to without the use of an automobile." Ideally, those who attempt to initiate Christian community would do so within a pedestrian-scaled neighborhood.

Because we at Pantego Bible Church knew this would be too aggressive a transition for the entire congregation to make overnight (and we honestly weren't even sure it would work), we created two larger geographic boundaries for our congregation to experience. We have experimented with an elementary school district as a boundary for community, as well as the high school district. Life in most communities has some tie to these geographic boundaries. We knew these would fall short of the pedestrian-scaled neighborhood we ultimately envisioned, but as pastors we wanted to provide a realistic alternative—one we felt would move people toward the community experience they were longing for.

Robert Putnam suggests that every ten minutes of commuting reduces social capital by 10 percent.[4] This is a profound conclusion that has a more far-reaching impact on community than most of us have ever considered. As we ponder this, we gain insight into why Americans are being robbed of community. It is not unusual for many people to use up their discretionary time commuting from one world of activities and events to another; for some this can represent twelve to thirty hours a week of car time. But we also know that most Americans, including Christians, are not about to store their cars in the garage anytime soon.

FROM AFFINITY TO NEIGHBORHOOD

When I came to Pantego Bible Church in 1990, we installed the large group, midsize group, and small group experience I described in chapter 6. From day one, we have organized our small groups under the management of our midsize group. However, these groups were initially formed by affinity, age category, or life stage, and not on the basis of neighborhoods. For example, all the young married people gathered in one group, while seniors gathered in another, regardless of where they lived. Because affinity gatherings are more comfortable and initially more appealing for the average church member, we knew a transition to a neighborhood model would be difficult. However, we also knew that affinity groups scattered throughout a twenty-mile radius do not work very well in creating true community. Therefore, over a period of several years we have shifted our people to a geographic model. We have supported Home Groups that were formed in a geographic area as large as a high school district, but we have progressively encouraged our people to move these groups into the preferred geographic density of a pedestrian-scaled neighborhood.

While we have not completely accomplished this assignment for the entire congregation, we have a large number of neighborhood communities that have developed and are producing profound results. The difficulty is convincing people of something they have never experienced. Once they try it, they get it—but getting them to try it is a hard sell. Yet the growing number of converts is doing more to help this transition than any sermon I've given on the topic. Their enthusiasm for what they have found in neighborhood community is contagious. Listen to the testimony of one family who made the transition from life-stage small groups to neighborhood-based community:

> As new Christians, we were eager to join a Community Group of couples who were in the same life stage as we were. Once we had joined a Community Group, we were invited to participate in a Growth Group and were excited to become a part of a small group of believers who could help us grow. Over the next few months, our experience with our small group meetings became frustrating. We met every other week to exchange prayer requests and pray about each other's intimate issues. The distance between our homes (across town) meant that we rarely had contact with each other between meetings. We had little "down time" to simply chat and develop true friendships.
>
> Our shift to join a Neighborhood Home Group was motivated primarily by convenience. We no longer had to drive fifteen to thirty minutes each way, with small children in tow, to meet with our small group. However, many other benefits soon became obvious. Now we are in a small group with families who live within a mile of our house; we see each other frequently—at the grocery store, school, or simply out walking. We meet spontaneously at the park or help each other with small favors. Our children are developing close relationships, even across age differences. Home Group meetings have become the highlight of our week.
>
> What started three years ago as five families meeting each Sunday evening has grown to approximately twenty families meeting in three groups, all within the

same elementary school zone. Several months ago all three Home Groups began meeting together on Sunday mornings as a midsize Community Group to participate in Bible study and instruction. This is the key to keeping continuity among multiple Home Groups. God has allowed us to participate in his glory as a community of believers where we have witnessed amazing events. By simply responding to needs as we learn about them, we are participating or have participated in the following:

- We prayed and provided meals for a neighborhood family. We learned that the wife/mother was diagnosed with cancer and was beginning her chemotherapy. Her cancer is in remission, and they are now participating in a Home Group and attending our church on Sunday morning.
- We provide a monthly birthday party for residents of a local "assisted-living center."
- Annually we provide backpacks and sort school supplies for a local Christian charity.
- Weekly we participate in the church's "parking ministry," greeting and directing new families and singles to the church building on Sunday morning.
- We faithfully support each other with meals and care.

We are constantly amazed at the many ways God allows us to participate in his work. Our experiences have not happened because we set out to find a need; they happened because of the availability of our group to be used in our neighborhood as God opened up needs to us. We were able to respond because of our level of commitment to each other, which is fostered by the frequency and closeness of our contact with each other.

Our children participate in all that we do, and they are witnessing God working through the united response of friends in a small group (the body of Christ). We are experiencing true biblical community—and we believe that geographical closeness is a vital element that works!

THE GEOGRAPHIC INFRASTRUCTURE

Below is a chart that describes how we currently organize ourselves.

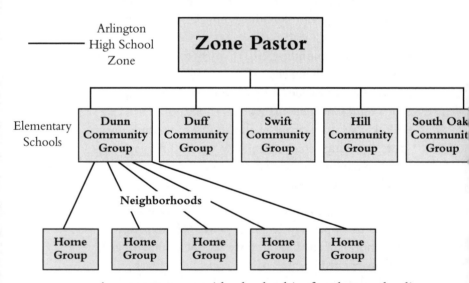

THE CONNECTING CHURCH INFRASTRUCTURE

A *zone pastor* provides leadership for those who live within the boundaries of a particular high school district. In the example above, the zone pastor oversees the Arlington High School District. His goal is to develop five to seven midsize Community Groups that will meet on Sunday morning. These Community Groups form within specific elementary school districts. For example, within the Arlington High School district there are eight elementary schools. So, a Community Group would be formed for the Dunn Elementary School area, one for the Duff Elementary School area, and so forth.

The Community Groups are led by volunteer leaders we call *Community Group shepherds*. The principal job of the zone pastor is to recruit, train, and oversee Community Group shepherds. The goal is for fifty people who live within a particular elementary school area (the Duff Elementary School area, for example) to become a part of this midsize group. If the group grows beyond this size, we start a new group, always looking to create more densely populated geographic boundaries.

Home Groups are gatherings of ten people who live in a neighborhood. All Home Groups fall under the authority and leadership of the Community Group in their elementary school district. There are a maximum of seven Home Groups for each Community Group. For example, the Duff Elementary School Community Group has a Home Group of people who live in the Waggoner Drive neighborhood. A volunteer Home Group leader, who is under the authority of the Duff Community Group shepherd, leads the Waggoner Home Group.

REPRODUCTION

As groups grow to the maximum size, they must reproduce themselves into other groups. Like many other churches, we have leaders-in-training at all levels. Ideally, the Home Group leader has a leader-in-training, the Community Group shepherd has a leader-in-training (usually one of his Home Group leaders), and a zone pastor has a leader-in-training (usually one of his Community Group shepherds). When the time comes to launch a new Home Group, Community Group, or Zone, the leadership is in place to make it happen.

This model of ministry can work, whether your church consists of a hundred members or ten thousand members. The pastor of a church of one hundred people might start out recruiting two Community Group shepherds to lead two midsize geographic groups. These Community Group shepherds can then recruit five to seven Home Group leaders to establish the small group experience. When the number of Community Groups grows to seven, the pastor will need to hire an additional person to do what he does in overseeing the Community Group shepherds. Often this person is one of the Community Group shepherds who has done well in his duties, is sufficiently trained in theology, and feels passionate enough about the role of a zone pastor that he is willing to make a career change.

Typically, the senior pastor would maintain four Community Groups under his authority while the newly hired zone pastor would take three. At this point the church attendance in midsize groups should be roughly seven hundred adults. As the number of midsize groups grows to fourteen, two additional pastors need to be hired—one to handle expansion growth, the other to take over the senior pastor's role as a zone pastor. At this point the senior pastor takes responsibility to oversee the three zone pastors. Once the number of zone pastors reaches five, the senior pastor must bring in what we call a "district pastor" to properly manage the zone pastors so that his own ministry can be focused on visioning and preaching. Keep in mind that at this point the church is averaging 1,750 adults participating in midsize groups!

Children and Youth

You may recall from chapter 6 that our children and youth ministries also follow the same format as our adult ministries. There is a large group gathering, a midsize group gathering, and small group gatherings, and the ministries focus on the spiritual growth of the individual child or student. We have also positioned these groups into the same geographical zones. The implications are staggering!

Our Student Ministries (fifth grade to twelfth grade) have midsize group gatherings, also called Community Groups, based on school zones. Instead of meeting on Sunday morning, these groups meet on Wednesday evenings. They are drawn together on the basis of the school the student attends. If the teenager attends Arlington High, they go to the Arlington High Community Group on Wednesday night; if the teenager goes to Mansfield High, they gather in that geographic area on Wednesday night, and so on. We have about twenty high schools within our serviceable area. We do the same for students in our junior high schools.

Our children also congregate by geographic zones. The children's midsize gathering is on Sunday morning. When the boys and girls come into the large room, they immediately go to the area where their school is represented. We recruit *zone shepherds* to oversee a high school area that usually includes five to seven elementary schools. These can be paid staff people or volunteers. In our church, interns who are preparing for full-time professional ministry fulfill this role.

I mentioned earlier that our ministry seeks to integrate adults, youth, and children at the Home Group level, whereas most churches confine their integration efforts to the worship service setting. In chapter 14 I will explain in more detail how we accomplish this integration into the Home Group. The point to be made here is that the small group experience for youth and children is also geographical.

CHURCH GROWTH STRATEGIES

In America the typical pastor feels enormous pressure to produce numerical growth. Because of this reality, pastors are compelled to ask whether this neighborhood model of community can produce church growth as we have traditionally defined it. Consider the findings of Christian sociologist and church consultant Lyle Schaller. In his book *Discontinuity and Hope,* Schaller presents this stunning discovery:

> Back in the 1950s it was relatively easy to find a church in rural or small-town America in which one-third or more of the local residents were constituents. That could be 30 percent of the several hundred residents living within three or four miles of the meeting place. The open country church might include more than one-half of the nearby households as members.[5]

But as I have noted in this section, things have changed dramatically for neighborhoods and for the churches that served them. Schaller makes this observation:

> The combination of the erosion of inherited institutional loyalties, the widespread ownership of the private motor vehicle, good roads, the growth of individualism, the increased geographical separation of the place of work from the place of residence, and the growing competition for the loyalty of the consumer has transformed American society. One result of that is the replacement of the small neighborhood worshiping community by the large regional church.[6]

How has the large regional church done numerically, compared to the neighborhood church? Well, if you were to walk into one of the fast-growing regional churches in the American suburbs, you might see thousands of people; from this you would naturally conclude that the regional megachurch has done a better job of reaching their community than the neighborhood church—but this is simply not the case. Schaller states that the "replacement model" in new church development reaches somewhere between 0.5 percent to 2 percent of the residents who live within ten to twenty miles of the meeting place.[7] For example, a church that has 1,250 to 2,500 worshipers is considered a large and successful church. However, the total number of people who live in the area surrounding this church can be, and often is, 250,000 people—or perhaps even more. Running the calculation, we see that they are reaching 0.5 percent to 1 percent of their community.

When developers unwittingly built suburbs on the outskirts of small downtowns, in effect causing their slow death, church leaders were by and large unaware that they were being robbed of their best strategy for reaching people. What was the key to that tried-and-true strategy? Schaller suggests that "the most significant consequence of this overall trend can be condensed into one word. Focus."[8] In other words, concentrated efforts in smaller geographic boundaries can produce greater results.

REINVENTING CHURCH

How do the above facts affect the way we should "do church" in the twenty-first century? I feel called by God to serve the people in the suburban sprawl of the Dallas–Fort Worth, Texas, area. Therefore, I am committed to staying put, even though I know that the structure of our metropolis militates against the creation of community. And yet, based on what I now know about community, what if I tried to reinvent the neighborhood church within the regional church I pastor?

Our church sits on a beautiful seventy-six-acre site centrally located between Fort Worth and Dallas. Because of our highly attractive freeway location, we have access to over 1.5 million people within a twenty-minute drive of our campus. Reaching 1 percent of the 1.5 million, or fifteen thousand people, is an achievable goal but not nearly as exciting as the 30 percent rate achieved by the neighborhood church in the early to middle years of the twentieth century. If we created neighborhood-based subcongregations within our regional church, with decentralized zone pastors, care structures, outreach programs, and the like, could we possibly beat this "glass ceiling" that most suburban churches experience?

While it may be too early to tell whether this will work, let me share my own experience with community. Two and half years ago, my family moved into a neighborhood with eighty-eight homes. There were two Christian families living in the neighborhood who attended our church. We approached them with our ideas about community and went to work on the principles laid out in this book. Today we have fifteen families from our neighborhood (and from our church) fully involved in community. That's 17 percent of the total households! What is even more exciting is that many of these families were previously unchurched or even non-Christians. On top of that, we currently have relationships, or at least acquaintances, with up to 50 percent of our neighbors. We know almost 100 percent of everyone by name.

In his work *Diffusion of Innovations*, Everett Rogers suggests that if 16 percent of a defined constituency adopts a new way of doing things, it creates a movement.[9] The odds are in favor of the innovation—that in time upwards to 86 percent of the total population will adopt this new way of thinking and living. I don't know of any suburban church that has reached 17 percent of its households located within its area.

I believe it is possible to borrow from the focused effectiveness of the neighborhood church of days gone by and insert it within the regional church model. Our neighborhood is now made up of three Home Groups. The people in the Home Groups are a part of a midsize Community Group in our elementary school area under the leadership of a full-time zone pastor. In addition, we are just one of several neighborhoods within our larger regional church structure to experience this kind of growth. We are certainly committed to this strategy until another model emerges that promises to reach people for Christ and transform them into fully developing followers of Christ in the context of authentic biblical community.

Can we really reinvent community in an age of individualism, or should we just accept these contemporary cultural conditions as a permanent reality? Social and political scientist Robert Putnam is optimistic about our chances for change. He cites another time in American history where we were faced with the same kind of social recession that threatens community today—a time when we were successful in reinventing ourselves. Many call this period "the Progressive Era," which took place roughly between 1900 and 1915. American industrialism was having a similar impact on community then as technology is having on ours today.

Speaking not about church health but about the broader issue of civic restoration, Putnam suggests that the church played a key role. In a chapter titled "Lessons of History: The Guilded Age and the Progressive Era," Putnam writes the following:

> Although the culture of industrial America was becoming in some respects more secular, religion played a substantial role in the civic revitalization of the period, quite

apart from the devotional activities of local parishes and congregations. The Salvation Army, an evangelical Protestant movement ministering to the unchurched urban poor with missionary zeal and unorthodox mass-marketing—marches, brass bands, and "Hallelujah lassies"—spread from Britain to America in 1880.[10]

Suggesting that organizations and activities like these were the epoch for the "muscular Christianity" that reacted against individualism, Putnam cites Henry Ward Beecher's admonition to seminarians at Yale to "multiply picnics" in their parishes.[11] Churches took this and other such charges and employed them in their battle to overcome the devastating effects of industrialism on the human need for community.

We can once again return to a way of living that promotes authentic community, but it will take new and creative strategies rooted in the historical wisdom passed down from insightful sages and even ordinary people. If we continue to apply the same old strategies in our cities and churches that we've used for the past fifty years, we should not expect to achieve different results. If you believe that the words in this book impart some semblance of wisdom about biblical community, then I invite you to join me in the exciting mission of reinventing the church!

PART 3

CONNECTING TO COMMON POSSESSIONS

11

THE PROBLEM OF CONSUMERISM

The breakdown of a common purpose and a common place over the last fifty years has embedded individualism as a way of life in America, as well as in most modern communities around the world. Without warning or desire, individualism has bred the most intense isolation since the day Adam spent alone on the sixth day of creation.

Now one more obstacle to community raises its ugly head out of the modal qualities of individualism and isolation, namely, *consumerism*. Consumerism is about consumption—the concentrated effort to consume things in order to meet one's real and perceived needs and wants. While in its basic form consumption is both necessary and permissible, when it is practiced in an environment where the individual is sovereign, it can easily become an imbalanced obsession that kills community.

One of consumerism's driving principles is *rights over responsibility*. In this system, the pursuit and protection of one's rights always wins out over one's responsibility to his or her neighbor. It's not something people deliberately choose because they are more depraved than previous generations; it is a natural consequence of individualism. When community life is strong, everyone looks out for each other. We are our "brother's keeper." When individualism reigns as the predominant way of life, there is no one to look out for you. You must take on this role for yourself, and it is a full-time job.

Under both modes of life, the Golden Rule applies, but it is defined and applied very differently. Under community, the Golden Rule says, "Do to others as you would have them do to you."[1] Under consumerism, the Golden Rule says, "Do to others before they do one to you"—or even more instructive, "He who has the gold, rules." The notion is simple: the more cash you have, the better positioned you are to protect your rights. Logically then, under a community philosophy, *Christ* is at the center of our lives as the driving motivation and resource for the biblical definition of the Golden Rule. Under the consumerism philosophy, *money* is at the center of our lives as the driving motivation and resource for the latter definition of the Golden Rule. Jesus said that these two philosophies cannot coexist; one will win out against the other.[2] The power of culture is tipped so strong toward individualism that it makes it very difficult for the Christian to sustain an allegiance to Christ. We claim Christ as Lord, but our actions of loving God and our neighbor are usually subservient to our own needs and wants. Many even find themselves looking to God to serve and sanctify their consumerism.

Thus, consumerism is not only a result of isolation, it also funds or fuels the continuation of the "sovereign individual" ideology. Consider this depiction of the effects of these cultural characteristics:

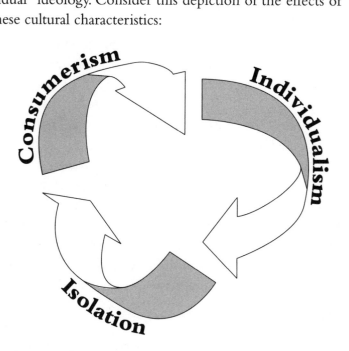

As a result, consumerism seeks to curb the negative feelings of isolation; we spend increasing amounts of money in an attempt to feel better. However, the more we are obsessed about applying consumerism as a solution to our loneliness, the more it feeds the individualism mindset. It's a vicious cycle.

CONSUMERISM AND COMMUNITY

We have discovered that consumerism, in combination with individualism and isolation, can have a devastating effect on our attempts to build genuine community. Consumerism undermines community in at least four significant ways.

Imbalanced Independence

Consumerism in a strong economy tempts a kind of independence that can quickly diminish community. John Locke puts it succinctly when he writes, "If we needed things we couldn't buy, many of us would have more friendships."[3] The pursuit and attainment of Western wealth has enabled us to bypass each other as we pursue meeting our basic needs. Poet and farmer Wendell Berry says, "If people don't need each other, they will spend little time together telling stories to each other, and if they don't know one another's stories, how can they know whether or not to trust one another?"[4] This experience of not needing each other leads us to the second way in which consumerism destroys community.

Distrust

Our isolation creates a distorted view of the people who live around us. Polls would suggest that only 16 percent of the people who live around us are truly immoral.[5] However, if these are the only people we meet on the nightly news on the television, it gives us the perspective that everyone is immoral and is seeking to take advantage of us. We then begin to view everyone through suspicious eyes. We begin to assume that friendliness from a stranger comes with a self-promoting agenda. Consequently, because we don't know most of the people we run into in public places, we look at them with distrust. With this attitude as our starting point, our chances of achieving true community become squelched.

Lawsuits

Consumerism is driven by a preoccupation to meet one's needs and to protect one's property and rights—because, after all, if we don't, no one else will. Therefore, as a natural result, the filing of lawsuits has risen dramatically in the last fifty years. The community ideology Jesus promoted suggests that if someone asks you to walk one mile with them, go two; if someone wants to sue you and take your tunic, let him have your cloak as well; if someone slaps you on the cheek, turn and offer him the other.[6] The teachings of the apostle Paul on lawsuits are almost passé today:

> *If any of you has a dispute with another, dare he take it before the ungodly for judgment instead of before the saints? Do you not know that the saints will judge the world? And if you are to judge the world, are you not competent to judge trivial cases? Do you not know that we will judge angels? How much more the things of this life! Therefore, if you have disputes about such matters, appoint as judges even men of little account in the church! I say this to shame you. Is it possible that there is nobody among you wise enough to judge a dispute between believers? But instead, one brother goes to law against another—and this in front of unbelievers!*
>
> *The very fact that you have lawsuits among you means you have been completely defeated already. Why not rather be wronged? Why not rather be cheated? Instead, you yourselves cheat and do wrong, and you do this to your brothers.*[7]

Many people who read these words would consider this concept naive and almost Pollyannaish. By no means! In these words are rich principles filled with life, love, and community for those who obey them. They seem ridiculous only because they are built on a foundation different from individualism and unabashed consumerism. Ultimately, distrust and lawsuits kill the very economy that feeds consumerism. Long-lasting economic development is built on trust, win-win proposals, and sacrifices—which are bedrock truths of community.

Social Loafing

When community is wounded and a culture of individualism takes over, people stop looking out for each other. When this happens, as it has in America, the needs of the poor, the homeless, and the broken go unmet. In the absence of self-sacrificial love for one's neighbor, the government is forced to step in and help. To run these programs they must tax the people. As it turns out, these government-funded programs are often initiated with good motives but typically produce poor results. Even worse, the person who could be an effective servant and who could be part of the solution for a hurting person is encouraged by these programs to have a mind-set that says, "I pay taxes for the government to take care of this!"—he or she has contracted the disease John Locke calls "social loafing."[8] Rigor mortis sets in to our muscles of human justice and kindness; sadly, this kind of sedentary apathy is difficult to reverse in a culture of consumerism.

LIFE-STAGE MARKETING

A culture of consumerism requires the presence of vendors who, under the modality of individualism, will mar-

ket to the needs of the individual. The products and services they offer, undergirded by intense marketing horse-
power, seek to feed our egos and satisfy our perceived
needs and wants. But in the end they also divide us. Rarely
does the American family do things together. Everyone gets
divided up into some kind of a market segment—so much
so that the family nucleus is not a simple community but a
detached collection of individuals. The church in the last
fifty years, as a whole, has played right into this method. By
and large, successful churches are not really building community, but they are doing a great job of marketing con-
sumable services to individuals.

The Johnson family can easily admit they are caught up
in consumerism. You see, it is the only logical strategy in
our culture of individualism. Consumerism is not based on
the amount of money you have to spend but the way you
think about the amount of money you have to spend. They
have lived under the grip of this lifestyle long enough to
feel the negative effects mentioned.

In many other parts of the world the idea of success is
a quiet dinner with friends, telling stories and sharing
laughter and life together. In America the idea of success is
accumulating more things. The former strategy leads people
toward community, whether it is based on Christian principles or not; the latter strategy leads people away from
community in pursuit of working longer hours to earn
more money so you can purchase that thing that promises
contentment—but, of course, never delivers.

When the things we have just purchased do not bring
about satisfaction from our isolation and our loneliness, we
begin to look at others who, on the outside, appear happier

and have more, or better, things than we do. We then set a goal to purchase still more items—more often than not by plunking down our credit cards, in a worthy effort to feel whole. The Bible says that covetousness, evil desires, greed, and such things are idolatry.[9] When we pursue as our means of fulfillment the things our neighbor possesses instead of pursuing God, we worship these things rather than God alone. Now we see in full bloom that covetousness and greed also rob us of community. Instead of pursuing the joy of a conversation, we pursue the purchase of pieces of plastic or metal in varying sizes. This pursuit pulls us away from the time-consuming pursuit of community. The popular quotation sums it up well, proclaiming that we "love things and use people instead of loving people and using things."

Given the current condition of our society, it will take great courage and intentionality to live a different way— because to do so means we will have to be countercultural. Speaking from an architectural, urban-planning point of view, editor Philip Langdon offers this pessimistic prediction for the future:

> It will not be easy to bring this vision of suburban design to fruition. The idea of a compact, mixed, affordable, pedestrian-scale community has emerged at a time when there is still a great deal of wealth in the United States, especially in the top fifth of the population. Surplus wealth enables people to persist in building wasteful, inadequate communities and then compensate for the communities' failings by buying private vehicles and driving all over the metropolitan area in search of what ought to be available close to home. The satisfying com-

munity designs of earlier times were dictated to a considerable extent by scarce resources. People supported neighborhood stores, and relied on sidewalks to get to and from the stores, because they didn't have the money and cars that would allow them to shop at big stores dispersed along distant roads. People lived at higher densities—and enjoyed a robust neighborhood life—because they could not afford detached houses on large lots in subdivisions many miles from their place of work. People settled in compact, relatively self-sufficient communities because the economy permitted little extravagance. One complication for today's traditionalists, then, lies in advocating a more efficient, compact community before the economy has made it necessary for the nation as a whole to adopt such a thrifty outlook. Thus it is possible that most suburban development in the United States will continue for some time on the profligate course it has followed since the Second World War.[10]

On a more positive note, Christianity and the Christian church have a long history of overcoming obstacles and swimming against the current. Bob and Karen Johnson are Christians—thus, they have the power within them *through Christ* to make it happen. If you are a devoted follower of Christ, so do you.[11]

Now on to practical solutions.

12

SHARING COMMON POSSESSIONS

There is a solution to recommend to the Johnson family as an exceedingly rich alternative to consumerism—one best described in the writings of Luke as he peers into the community of the first-century Christians, and as his gaze locks particularly on a man named Barnabas:

> *All the believers were one in heart and mind. No one claimed that any of his possessions was his own, but they shared everything they had. With great power the apostles continued to testify to the resurrection of the Lord Jesus, and much grace was upon them all. There were no needy persons among them. For from time to time those who owned lands or houses sold them, brought the money from the sales and put it at the apostles' feet, and it was distributed to anyone as he had need.*
>
> *Joseph, a Levite from Cyprus, whom the apostles called Barnabas (which means Son of Encouragement), sold a field he owned and brought the money and put it at the apostles' feet.*[1]

In direct contrast is the story that immediately follows.

Now a man named Ananias, together with his wife Sapphira, also sold a piece of property. With his wife's full knowledge he kept back part of the money for himself, but brought the rest and put it at the apostles' feet.[2]

The problem with Ananias and Sapphira wasn't that they hadn't turned over the full proceeds from their land sale; the problem was that they gave everyone the impression they had given it all when in fact they hadn't. They wanted the public glory of being sacrificial givers for the sake of others, but when the truth came out, their own selfishness was at the core of their motive.

This is a poignant peek into the darkness of consumerism. On the outside, the actions of Ananias and Sapphira may have looked like community and selflessness, but it was clear that, on the inside, their actions were motivated by selfish gain. Let each of us in our own heart before God determine whether our acts of kindness are like the acts of Barnabas or like those of Ananias and Sapphira. We do not begin to experience true community just because people give up their resources for others. But when people give up their resources because the power of the resurrection of Jesus Christ has penetrated their lives, it overwhelms them with the grace of giving.

The final solution to authentic Christian community is *common possessions*—"No one claimed that any of his possessions was his own, but they shared everything they had."[3] Now, this does *not* mean they simply pooled all their resources together. It appears that everyone maintained ownership of their particular possessions, but they were more than willing to share or sell what they had so that those in need would be cared for. The mind-set that must be adopted is this: All that we are, everything that we own, belongs to God (see page 76). He is the owner; we are merely the managers, the stewards. Our goal is to be open to God's leadership in terms of how he wants us to use his resources, including how he wants us to spend our very lives. What would Jesus want me to do with this car, swimming pool, lawn mower, extra cash, and the like. Without question, these will be the toughest adjustments to make as we begin to look at life through a different set of spectacles.

In his *Context* newsletter, Martin Marty quoted the late Yale professor-preacher Halford Luccock:

> You remember that among the Franks, whole armies were sometimes given baptism at one stroke, and many warriors went into the water with their right hands held high so that they did not get wet. Then they could say, "This hand has never been baptized," and they could swing their battle axes just as freely as ever. The modern counterpart of that partial baptism is seen in many people who have been baptized, all except their pocketbooks. They held these high out of the water.[4]

Many Christians today hold their wallets out of the water so they can continue, in their own minds, to maintain ownership over and control of their possessions and continue to accumulate more possessions. Now, I do not want to suggest that God doesn't want Christians to have money, to seek to earn more money, or even to enjoy what some might call "elaborate" possessions. As long as these things have been secured within biblical and ethical boundaries and the follower of Christ is devoting his or her time and talents to that which they truly believe God is leading them to do, God will be honored. What is of utmost importance here is commitment to the principle that "man does not live on bread alone, but on every word that comes from the mouth of God."[5] Our guiding principles must be based on the understanding that Jesus is "the bread of life."[6]

Once again, it all comes down to putting Christ at the center of your life over against money. Money and possessions are to be seen as tools and resources given to us by God to be used to achieve his objectives. Think of the man or woman who owns a company but decides to turn over ownership to someone who has greater resources and capital—while he or she stays on as the general manager or president. This is how our relationship with God works as far as our worldly assets. He is the owner with far greater resources than we could ever dream of possessing—and we are the CEO.

Christian stewardship, or life management, does not involve just money and physical possessions. God wants all of our gifts, our talents, and our time. When people make this kind of commitment to God in the context of true community, it is a sight to behold.

Five Characteristics of Community Around Common Possessions

I want to suggest that there are at least five common characteristics present among effective places of community when the principles of stewardship, or common possessions, are applied:

Interdependency

In American society, the goal and dream has become *independence*. Even when we work with the poor, often our goal is to make them independent, just like we are. Independence is a self-sufficiency, usually accompanied by an adequate cash flow, that enables us to function in life without the aid of others. While the proverb "Give a person a fish and you feed him for a day; teach a person how to fish and you feed him for a lifetime" is a helpful one, we must be careful not to apply it for the purpose of helping another person become independent but rather for the purpose of helping them become a contributing member of an *interdependent* community.

Social programs that keep people *dependent* on "picking up their fish each day" are not prospering in meeting their objective of showing effective compassion—but neither is it wise to promote unmitigated independence. The air of independence encourages and fuels individualism, isolation, and consumerism. Interdependent persons are usually those who could, by nature of their plentiful resources and strong health, be independent but rather choose to make their resources available to others—instead of choosing to consume all they can for themselves, either through accumulating vast savings or through purchasing all kinds of amenities.

Paul summarizes this mind-set in his letter to the Corinthians, who lived in the booming and progressive country of Greece:

> *Our desire is not that others might be relieved while you are hard pressed, but that there might be equality. At the present*

time your plenty will supply what they need, so that in turn their plenty will supply what you need. Then there will be equality, as it is written: "He who gathered much did not have too much, and he who gathered little did not have too little."[7]

For the Johnsons adopting this perspective will mean that they will look at their current resources (money, possessions, time, and talents) and together evaluate how God would want them to use these resources to show love for God and for neighbor. This attitude will also serve as a filter through which they will pass future decisions about how they spend their time and what they purchase. Now, instead of always asking what would make *them* happy, they are principally concerned with what would please God— and it is sometimes amazing to see how God will often smile at us and nudge us to "treat" ourselves to things that bring us great pleasure. We are his children, after all, and he truly delights to see us enjoy life. Yet, more than anything, he wants us to be obedient.[8]

The formula is simple: Truly delight yourself in God, "and he will give you the desires of your heart."[9] If you choose to do this, one of two things will happen: Either you will find that, as you grow in your love for and delight in God, he will change that which you desire, or out of the pleasure he derives from your spiritual maturity and trustworthiness, he will give you that which brings you pleasure. One of the reasons God may not give us greater responsibility at work, open the way for us to get larger raises, or provide us with more possessions is because we have not proven to be trustworthy stewards with what he has already given us: "From everyone who has been given much, much will be demanded; and from the one who has been entrusted with much, much more will be asked."[10]

In the Old Order Amish communities in Ohio and Pennsylvania, interdependence is valued. When a barn needs to be built, the family does not flaunt its independence and success by hiring out the labor to a contractor. Rather, they organize a "barn raising." Everyone in the community comes together to share a big meal and to build the barn. Because many Amish men are skilled craftsmen who are in high demand in the non-Amish suburbs, they could afford to outsource many of their projects. But they choose not to, because it would undermine and diminish their community, which is a far more important value to them. I'm not implying that there is something wrong with outsourcing; the problem comes when it robs us of the opportunity to experience authentic community.

The average American *can* build a life for themselves in which they don't need anyone—but they *shouldn't*. If we are going to experience true community we must choose to be *interdependent* with others. Negotiating this value in an era of abundant wealth will be difficult, but it is essential to do so if we want to find fulfillment in our search to belong. Writer James Howard Kunstler sums it up this way: "Community is not something you have, like a pizza, it is a local organism based on a web of interdependencies."[11]

Intergenerational Life

Another dynamic characteristic found among inspiring places of community is *intergenerational life.* In all places of effective community, with the possible exception of college life, the various strata of generations spend both structured and spontaneous time together. Intergenerational life isn't a luxury to be tried just to see if we like it—if it's "cool." No, it is essential in order for members of true community to grow as individuals and as members of one fellowship.

This really does make sense. There are the elderly, many of whom are grandparents; there are middle-aged parents and young parents; there are single adults and young adults; and then there are the precious children. Each has so much to offer the other. The child instills a wonderful sense of purpose into the older generations—encouraging them to serve as those who dispense the lessons of life they have learned over the years. The young single person renews our passion for spirited ideals, vision, and hope. What's more, they're also wonderful mentors for our children, because they have the energy to just "hang with them," and our children tend to look up to them. The parents carry the responsibility of being the principal providers and guides for their children. And finally, the elderly have so much to offer. Because they have learned so much about life, and have by and large been set free from the tyranny of the daily "To Do" list, they can look at life from a broad, global perspective and offer to all the wisdom built on their many years of personal experience.

Christian community is not an occasional group get-together led by small group leaders; it is at its core a familial structure. It is patriarchal and matriarchal in structure. It is something one is trained to participate in, by those who are older, over the course of life through all the stages of life.[12] However, because we have tended to be segmented into tightly defined life-stage groupings, even in the church, this view of community will require an unusual type of training—one never meant to be taught in the classroom but experienced throughout the course of everyday life.

Many church leaders still believe that the most effective grouping of people is centered around the sharing of a common life-stage experience. While it may be the fastest way to grow a group of people numerically, it is not going to produce the best qualitative results in the lives of individuals. Taking a group of young married couples who have small children, and putting these couples together in a room and expecting them to help each other navigate through these critical and sometimes exasperating years is a bit like asking a group of ten toddlers to brainstorm ways to cross a four-lane highway together.

The life-stage mind-set is so ingrained that it has a powerful effect both on the youngest members of our community as well as the oldest. As our children grow up, many are not comfortable in relating to people of other ages. Some refuse to play with anyone who is not within six months of their age. Furthermore, so devastating is life-stage grouping that according to recent reports, suicide among the elderly is at an all-time high.[13] It's painful to live without the kind of vital, lasting purpose that comes from being part of true community; it hurts not to belong!

Is it possible that we could see a cultural shift from life-stage community to intergenerational community at some point in our lifetime? Well, on the positive side, the growing value of intergenerational life is being recognized by young adults in their twenties; driven by postmodern values, they seem to be crying out for it. One Gen X couple is recorded as saying, "Our generation, without necessarily knowing it, is calling the church back to what the church has always been called to be—a multigenerational, multicultural, open, orthodox, and culturally engaged body of believers."[14] Dieter and Valerie Zander, pastors and baby-boomer mentors to Gen Xers, make this comment: "The potentially endless proliferation of new subgroups begins to look like it is based on nothing more substantial than catering to new styles. That kind of shallowness won't last."[15] Will the Gen Xers succeed in their quest? If I had to make a prediction, I would suggest that they will most likely live and die with the ideals—and not the reality. I believe the true cultural implementation lies within the experience of the children who are currently five years old or younger. By the time these kids are grandparents, intergenerational living could be established once again as the norm, at least for the Christian church community. Having said that, though, there is a real opportunity for those of us who are older to begin to build this mind-set into these children, to introduce them to the experiences of intergenerational community. The challenge we will encounter is to pass down a way of life to the next generation that we ourselves don't understand. Yet we must pick up the mantle and be pioneers of this ancient and trustworthy principle of community.

Once again we see that true community is countercultural. The bad news is that we may not see full societal adoption of this principle in our lifetime; the good news is we can begin to experience it for ourselves and for our children—if we want it badly enough!

Children

Closely related to the characteristic of intergenerational community life, but significant enough to earn its own discussion, is the role of *children* in community. Effective places of community accept the responsibility to effectively care for, nurture, and train its children.

Suburbs have created the "latchkey child." Movies such as *Suburbia* depict the tragic reality of isolation experienced by children who live in America's suburbs. In the absence of being provided for by their family, some kids respond by creating their own community—it's called a *gang,* and it's a community united around mostly unhealthy purposes. Yet it has clearly proven to create a sense of belonging for its members. For many gangs their choice of common place is the mall. Recently, in the Mall of America in Bloomington, Minnesota, several thousand teenagers who regularly congregate there became unruly and a 6:00 P.M. curfew was imposed. The associate general manager is quoted as saying that the reason they enacted the curfew was because "most kids just hang out, few shop."[16]

In the average American small group experience, children are by and large left out. (In some cases, group members may not be able to even name the children of fellow members.) The irony is that the kids are left with a babysitter so Mom and Dad can go to a small group to talk about their children. Ninety percent of the prayer requests made at the meeting center around either everybody's busy schedules or their concerns about their children. Sadly, many Christian children hate small group night.

In effective places of genuine Christian community, there are spiritual grandparents, aunts, uncles, cousins, nieces, and nephews—all of whom are intimately involved in the lives of the children. Indeed, it does take a village, a neighborhood, to raise a balanced and healthy child. We might well wonder whether we're looking to too many other things to serve as a substitute for wholesome intergenerational community. As long as we propagate dysfunctional families, it is conceivable that we will continue to propagate dysfunctional community.

When asked about including children in the small group experience, the response of most group members sounds like a broken record: "We tried it, and it didn't work." "It's too chaotic." "The adults don't enjoy it as much." The role of children in the life of the community is dismissed as though it were as optional as electric windows in a new vehicle. Well, it is *not* optional, and if we continue to ignore it, we will run the risk of seeing our children turn to other means of finding acceptance and fulfillment in their search to belong—things like involvement with drugs or with gangs.

Responsibility

In a culture of individualism, protecting one's own rights and meeting one's own needs reigns supreme. In a culture of true community, the opposite is true. While the individual certainly does, and should, take care of himself or herself in community, the priority is given to serving and caring for others. Biblical community is built on the words of the apostle Paul:

> If you have any encouragement from being united with Christ, if any comfort from his love, if any fellowship with the Spirit, if any tenderness and compassion, then make my joy complete by being like-minded, having the same love, being one in spirit and purpose. Do nothing out of selfish ambition or vain conceit, but in humility consider others better than your-selves. Each of you should look not only to your own interests, but also to the interests of others.
> Your attitude should be the same as that of Christ Jesus.[17]

When someone is suffering or is gripped by despair, the other members do not see their involvement as optional but as a duty that must be exercised if community is to work—and if it is to work for them when *they* are hurting. Remember, though, that the commitment to serve others is not made just because others will, in time, reach out to serve you. In Christ's community, where members are truly in fellowship with God, you are "supernaturally" led to the outpouring of love on others:

> This is how we know what love is: Jesus Christ laid down his life for us. And we ought to lay down our lives for our broth-ers. If anyone has material possessions and sees his brother in need but has no pity on him, how can the love of God be in him? Dear children, let us not love with words or tongue but with actions and in truth. This then is how we know that we belong to the truth, and how we set our hearts at rest in his presence whenever our hearts condemn us. For God is greater than our hearts, and he knows everything.[18]

Love for God and love for others go hand in hand. Followers of Christ just can't help expressing their love for God through loving others. What is growing in their hearts *must* find an external outlet. When we discover true community, the place where responsibility toward others is a higher priority than standing up for our own rights, we will never want to go back. It is so freeing when others look out for us, pick us up when we have fallen, genuinely applaud our accomplishments, and lovingly confront us when we career off the track. Self-promotion is ultimately a most unfulfilling and exhausting way to live.

Sacrifice

The final characteristic of the kind of community that promotes common possessions and negates consumerism is *sacrifice*. Sacrifice is responsibility taken to the next level—a painful and costly level. Most of the time we can execute responsibility in a way that does not challenge us; we merely draw on our physical, emotional, and financial reserves. From time to time, however, we are called on to dig deep into who we are and what we have so that in the end we become depleted in a significant way for the sake of someone else. Once again Eberhard Arnold says it well:

> In the human body, community is maintained only by the constant cycle of dying cells being replaced by new ones. In a similar way, a life of full community can take shape as an organism only where there is heroic sacrifice. Because it is an educational fellowship of mutual help and correction, of shared resources, and of work,

a true community is a covenant made in free-willing surrender and sacrifice. As such it fights for the existence of the church.[19]

It is at this point that effective Christian community breaks with effective non-Christian community. In order to achieve this objective of sacrificial service, one must truly be in fellowship with God; one must truly draw on the rich resources of the Holy Spirit within. When a great sacrifice has been made, the Christ-follower learns firsthand what Jesus meant when he said, "If anyone would come after me, he must deny himself and take up his cross and follow me. For whoever wants to save his life will lose it, but whoever loses his life for me will find it."[20]

In the late nineteenth century German social theorist Ferdinand Tonnies coined two words for community—*gemeinschaft* and *gesellschaft*. *Gemeinschaft* stands for the true community that flows from natural, emotional, and interdependent associations among people. It has become a catchphrase for the old "village community"—homogenous, interdependent, and close-knit. *Gesellschaft,* on the other hand, represents a contrived community characterized by the rational and instrumental associations we create. It is also a catchphrase for the impersonal, alienated, mobile, modern culture that has replaced *gemeinschaft*.[21] Sadly, many people will try to pawn off *gesellschaft* for *gemeinschaft*. Even the church does this (unknowingly for the most part). But as Eberhard Arnold suggests, "efforts to organize community artificially can only result in ugly, lifeless caricatures."[22]

The Johnsons have had all they can take of *gesellschaft;* they are ready for *gemeinschaft.* As we look in on them again, they are taking the plunge into biblical community. They know it won't be easy, but the alternative is year after year after year of the same lonely, unsatisfying experience. As they prepare to seek authentic community, they know they've been spared a great deal of loss and tragedy to this point in their lives. The next season of their life may very well include the care of aging parents and coping with the reality that one or both of their parents may die soon. They may have to deal with a major illness that strikes them or a family member, or perhaps they'll have to cope with the results of an accident. As their children enter the stage of adolescence, the Johnsons will need to adjust to the growing need for their kids to become independent. They worry about the possibility that an unstable economy could negatively affect their current situation of financial prosperity.

If and when these challenges come, the Johnsons simply do not want to face them alone. But they are driven by more than just needing to find comfort in the midst of the storms. They long for the joy that comes from being connected to the body of Christians in an authentic and rich way. They can sense that when their purpose in life is linked to the whole, they can achieve far more than what they could on their own. The Johnsons are coming to see the wisdom found in the lessons learned from the geese— that they can go 70 percent further each day by flying *together,* like a flock of geese in a V formation, than if they were to venture out on their own.

13

Rediscovering Interdependence

The time had come for the Johnsons. They had decided to give community a try. As they saw it, ultimately they had little to lose—but a great deal to gain. Their search to find a place of belonging was finally becoming a bigger priority than trying to outdo the Joneses in seeing who could purchase the most and the biggest things. While the Johnsons knew they could make minor adjustments in their lifestyle that would be helpful and make them feel less stressed and more comfortable, they wisely concluded that every principle of genuine community they chose to put aside would somehow diminish the quality and simplicity they were longing for so deeply.

It took several rounds of discussions at family meetings and much prayer, but they finally began to make aggressive moves toward pursuing their dream of community. They were profoundly motivated by the vision of the kind of life they would provide for their children; with that hope held out before them they courageously moved forward—even when the fear of change threatened to overwhelm them.

The first set of decisions Bob and Karen made was the toughest. They decided that over the course of six months Karen would make a transition from her current job to one she could do at home, using their home computer. Because of her accounting background, she was able to contract with two small businesses to keep their books. Although the salary was slightly smaller, the savings they realized in their gasoline and clothing budget nearly made up for it. A cut in salary was certainly worth the flexibility it offered and the time it freed up. The Johnsons were finding that while the automobile encourages mobility, technology could provide the opportunity for stability, if one chose to use it that way. (If not, technology will be just one more thing that clutters people's lives and causes them to run faster and faster.)

The second major step the Johnsons took was to move. They decided to downsize a bit and to make a fresh start in a new neighborhood. This time, however, they weren't just buying a house; they were buying a neighborhood. Three principles drove their decision: First, they set a price range that would allow them to fund the mortgage on Bob's salary alone; second, they looked for a neighborhood that would cut down the time of Bob's commute to work; third, they looked for a place where at least two families from their church lived. After they found a particular neighborhood that met all three criteria, they cautiously approached the two neighborhood families with their ideas about biblical community. Even though these families didn't fully understand all the principles the Johnsons had been searching out, they were craving more intimate friendships and a deeper personal walk with Christ for their family.

Everything was now lined up and ready to go. At the end of six months, Karen had made the transition to a home-based job that provided more flexibility; they sold their house and purchased a slightly smaller home that could be financed on Bob's salary; the location of the new home cut down Bob's daily commute to five minutes each way; and finally, and most important, they had found two families in their new neighborhood who were ready to give biblical community a real shot. Solution number one was established—*a common place.*

Then the Johnsons went to work on establishing their *common purpose.* They met with one of the pastors of their church and explained their mission—not sure how it would be received. To their immense satisfaction the pastor was not only supportive of the idea, but he also offered to help them along the way. None of the three families felt very literate when it came to Bible knowledge, so they met with the pastor on several occasions to study together. Finally, and with great enthusiasm, they all embraced the seven functions, or purposes, of biblical community described in chapter 5 (see pages 82–83):

S	**Spiritual Formation**
E	**Evangelism**
R	**Reproduction**
V	**Volunteerism**
I	**International Missions**
C	**Care**
E	**Extending Compassion**

They also embraced the set of beliefs, practices, and virtues built on Jesus' model of the Christian life (see pages 70–80). As they examined these biblical purposes, they were very excited about embarking on the journey and passing on a spiritual legacy to their children—but they were understandably overwhelmed. The three families agreed that the direction they were taking was the right one, and they decided simply to take it one day at a time. Bob drafted a covenant that laid out their common purpose; everyone, including the children from all three families, signed it. The structure was now in place, and they were on their way!

At the same time that the Johnsons were working on the structure of their newfound community, they also addressed the spontaneous side. They knew they needed to free up time to be at home and not be spending so much time in the car and at activities outside their neighborhood. By moving closer to Bob's work and eliminating Karen's commute altogether, an extra twelve hours a week was now available to them. After making a list of their activities and commitments, they began to say no to those that would pull them apart as a family and as a community—including "good" church activities and committee work. Instead of serving as members of the Missions Committee, they decided that they would support the church's missions projects by getting the three families directly involved.

With Karen's flexibility at home, she was now able to pick the children up from school and eliminate the expense of after-school care. On most nights the children could start and finish their homework by dinnertime. The Johnsons had set a goal to have dinner together as a family at least three times a week—and much to their surprise, they found that they were averaging four to six meals together a week.

The Johnsons had agreed that they would be available for each other and their neighbors from dinnertime through bedtime. Two to three times a week the Johnsons shared a meal or an after-dinner desert with the two Christian families in their neighborhood. They talked and laughed together; often they would nail down plans for getting together the next day or on the weekend—sometimes to watch a movie together on Friday evening, or to go on a men's golf outing or a campout, or to just take a leisurely stroll together through the neighborhood.

Bob and Karen also installed a big swing in their front yard. Several nights a week they would go outside with a cup of coffee or a glass of iced tea. Often they would play Frisbee or get a game of kickball going in the street. After a couple of weeks other neighbors began to wander over. The children were the first to come—asking their parents if they could play with the neighbors in their front yard, or maybe even in the street. The kids would have so much fun they couldn't be pulled away. Eventually, the parents would mosey over to take their kids home. In the process Bob and Karen were getting to know their neighbors. They really couldn't believe how simple it all was—and just how much they were enjoying it. They speculated that most of their new neighbors really wanted the same thing when it came right down to it, but were at a loss to know how to find it. Of all people, surely the Johnsons could identify. Thus, to begin to experience genuine community in their neighborhood was enormously satisfying to them.

THE BEST DAY OF THE WEEK

Sunday was the most important day for the Johnsons. It was the day the family and the community centered themselves spiritually. The day began at church. The Johnsons commented often on how much more meaningful the church experience had become since they embarked on this journey of authentic community. In the afternoon the family ate a light lunch. They agreed that Sunday would be a day where they would not work—no homework, no housework, no yard work, and no office work. It was a day for physical and spiritual replenishment and refreshment. On most Sunday afternoons Bob and Karen would, without apology, get an hour or an hour-and-a-half nap.

At 4:30 P.M. the family would get ready for Home Group. The three families rotated the task of hosting the gathering. At 5:00 they would arrive at the host's home. They gathered in a circle, held hands, and acknowledged the greatness and goodness of God and gave thanks for his provision of salvation, the community they enjoyed in Christ, and the wonderful food prepared by the three families. From 5:00–6:00 they shared a meal together. From 6:00–6:45 the families would assemble in the living room. They would review their covenant and sing a few worship songs. (One of the dads played the guitar, and on occasion the children who played instruments would join the band. It may not have always been beautiful, but it certainly brought big smiles to the faces of the parents as their children offered their instruments and talent to God in worship.)

After the worship time, typically there would be an opportunity for people to give a testimony of how God's grace was evident in their lives during the week. It might include the words of a thankful child, who tells of the answer to her prayer that God would help her in her test at school; it might include the testimony of an adult, who tells of how God was at work to teach him or her more about the love and faithfulness of the heavenly Father.

During the time of spiritual instruction, parents would take one of the thirty core beliefs, practices, and virtues from the Christian Life Profile and talk to their children about it (see pages 74–80). One week they might talk about the core belief of salvation by grace, and another week about the core virtue of gentleness. Each of the thirty biblical concepts has a creed, or affirmation statement, and a verse of Scripture that supports the idea. For example, one of the core beliefs in loving God has to do with our identity in Christ. The creedal statement affirms the following: "I am significant because of my position as a child of God." The Scripture verse that supports this foundational Christian belief is John 1:12–13: "Yet to all who received him, to those who believed in his name, he gave the right to become children of God—children born not of natural descent, nor of human decision or a husband's will, but born of God."

The parents and children are encouraged to memorize and meditate on all thirty concepts throughout the year. The Johnsons use their dinnertime during the week to learn the concepts and to reinforce the teachings. All thirty of the core beliefs, practices, and virtues from the Christian Life Profile are contained on a sheet that hangs on the refrigerator and can be pulled down each evening for review.

The Johnsons were ecstatic that they could finally do something tangible to build a spiritual framework in their children—something that would help them understand and experience the Christian life. They could now envision the day when their children went off to college or to the workplace and were challenged in their faith—when their own children and the children from the other families would stand strong because they would know what they believed and why they believed it, would practice their faith on a moment-by-moment basis, and would carry within them the virtuous fruit of the Spirit that brings so much inner joy and purpose. The Johnsons openly admitted that they were learning right along with their children. Better late than never! Their prayer was always that they would stay at least one step ahead of their children.

As the evening at Home Group progresses, the children would be dismissed around 6:45 for a time of playing together. In the Johnsons' group the ages of the children ranged from five to sixteen. All the kids enjoy playing together, and they are beginning to see each other as "spiritual cousins."

Before they join the rest of the kids, the teenagers usually go off by themselves for about fifteen minutes to do a devotional and share prayer requests. (At first, one of the teenage girls would occasionally complain that there was no one her exact age in Home Group. Her parents encouraged her to invite another neighborhood girl who went to the same school. What the parents didn't expect was that within a month after this girl began attending Home Group, the rest of the girl's family asked if they could come too. They were a Christian family who hadn't attended church for several years. The other three families and the pastor were all thrilled when this family began attending church services on Sunday morning.)

From 6:45–8:00 the adults would be together, concentrating on a particular purpose of the Seven Functions of Biblical Community (see pages 82-83). Each week afforded a different focus, planned in advance so everyone knew the topic. During this time the adults may update each other on their spiritual goals established through the use of the Christian Life Profile. They may spend a good portion of the evening praying for the spiritual, emotional, relational, and physical needs of their neighbors. On another evening they may plan the next compassion project, or actually go out, for example, and serve homeless families at the local shelter. At times the specific needs of the group will direct the focus. For example, if a group member is wrestling with a potential job change or a major illness of a family member, the adults might discuss the matter and then gather around the person or family and pray for them. In the descriptions below, I'll give more examples of how a Home Group might use their time together to fulfill the Christ-commanded purposes of the church.

Spiritual Formation

In addition to discussing one of the thirty core Christian concepts every week, Home Group members annually evaluate the area they believe they need to grow in, and they share it with the group. They would use an assessment tool based on the Christian Life Profile, which asks respondents first to evaluate themselves in each of the thirty facets (see pages 74–80) and then to give a questionnaire to three people who know them and love them. These three people are asked to evaluate the person only on the ten Core Virtues (joy, peace, hope, faithfulness, self-control, humility, love, patience, kindness/goodness, and gentleness). Each Home Group member compares his or her own personal evaluation with the other evaluations to target one core belief or practice they will focus on and one core virtue they want to develop further.

When Karen Johnson completed her profile, she discovered she was able to put Christian language to something she had been feeling for years: She struggles with the core virtue of *joy*. In particular, she came face-to-face with the fact that circumstances dictate her mood—a reality she saw, and something that Bob, her mother, and her sister saw in her as well. After further probing, she began to understand how this related to the low rating she had given herself on her core belief that God is truly a personal God—that he is involved in and cares about our daily lives, that he is in control of it all (see page 75).

Bob Johnson discovered that he struggled with the core virtue of *gentleness*—a struggle particularly evident in his inability to give people room to make mistakes. However, in his own personal evaluation of his core virtues, Bob had not been able to see this; rather, it was the consistent feedback of Karen, of his oldest child, and of a colleague from work that lovingly made him see that this virtue was a major challenge for him. This revelation hit Bob hard—but in a cathartic way. As he reexamined his belief in God's view of people (the core belief with regard to humanity), he realized that he didn't see people the way God sees them.

At Home Group one night, Bob and Karen agreed to share the results of their profile. For years their prayer requests had centered on their busy schedules, their joys and concerns about their children, and an occasional prayer for Aunt Martha's hip replacement. But now they were prepared to share something deeply personal and spiritual. They were terrified to become vulnerable, but they knew it was the right thing to do. That evening they discovered the joy of what has become in many respects a lost practice of biblical community, namely, the practice of *confession*.[1] As Bob and Karen opened up, the group members experienced a deeper expression of community. Bob and Karen concluded by asking the group to hold them accountable and to pray for them as they sought to grow in the grace of Christ in these specific areas. In the midst of tears all around, the most touching thing took place. As Karen finished sharing, all the women put their hands on her and prayed for her. Then Bob also went over and placed his arms on her shoulders and prayed for her, along with the other women. So moved were Bob and Karen that they both broke down and began to weep. They knew then that they had crossed a new threshold in their relationship with God and each other.

From this night forward Bob and Karen, as well as the other group members, not only began to speak about the areas they wished to grow in on their Christian journey, they also began to develop action steps to help them achieve their objectives. At every meeting thereafter, one person agreed to give an update on his or her progress, and the group would pray again for this person. Spiritual formation was beginning to take place in this little band of Christians who had covenanted together in biblical community.

Evangelism

The members of the Home Group knew that God wanted them to share their faith with their neighbors— something no one in the group had been comfortable doing before. In commitment to this biblical purpose, each household agreed to pray for three other households in the neighborhood. During their evening prayer time (a fifteen- to thirty-minute period of time), they would pray for these families by name. In addition, they committed to looking for opportunities to help these families and to share their faith with them. When they went for walks in the evening, they would often say a prayer as they passed these neigh-bors' homes. The group decided not to be pushy, but inten-tional. The grace of Christ just didn't seem to fit with the hard-sell approach.

It was a slow process but an effective one. As time went by, the other neighbors knew of the Home Group's exis-tence. Because the Home Group families spent a lot of time in their front yards and went back and forth to each others' homes so often, they became the best-known and most winsome neighbors on the block. Most people became naturally attracted to them—though a few raised their eyebrows in hesitation.

The Home Group members tried a wide variety of activities to reach out to neighbors. They planned a New Year's Eve "progressive dinner" party to which they invited all the neighbors. On Wednesday nights the men got together for pickup basketball games at a neighbor's house. The women scheduled an occasional evening out for dinner. Neighborhood children were routinely invited to join the other children at Home Group meetings on Sundays.

Home Group members soon realized that one of the most effective ways to engage a family was to invite them to come to a worship service at church. They discovered that 50 percent of the invited people would go just by virtue of receiving a simple invitation. Because their church's worship services were so biblically focused and so relevant to daily living, the members of the Home Group were almost certain that those they invited to come would enjoy it.

Everyone was incredibly excited when a neighborhood couple who had begun to attend church came to trust Christ as their Savior following a service where the pastor had delivered a clear message on the core belief of salvation by grace. The couple naturally (better to say, supernaturally) became a part of Bob and Karen's Home Group. They were grandparents who added a wonderfully rich diversity to the group.

For the first time in Bob and Karen's life they were evangelizing. Yet, it seemed so natural, so right. What a joy they were experiencing as they pointed others to the most significant transformation possible—new life through Jesus Christ.

Reproduction

Over the course of the first year, five other neighborhood families joined the Home Group, raising the total attendance, including children, to thirty-five people. The original three families had prepared for this day as they formed their covenant initially. After the first year, they began a new group. One of the other families had begun to help lead the group in preparation for this day, so the leadership was already in place. While it was difficult for everyone, in the end it restored the intimacy they were beginning to lose when more than thirty people gathered in one home. Two years after the beginning of the original group they started another group, because the new neighbors were joining the church and beginning to attend Home Group.

Bob and Karen met with the other Home Group leaders once a month for dinner to pray and to plan. On one occasion their pastor joined them and suggested that the three groups form a midsize group that would meet on Sunday morning. Everyone loved the idea. They decided to use the time to discuss the pastor's sermon, which had dealt with one of the thirty core beliefs, practices, and virtues from the Christian Life Profile.

The pastor later approached the Johnsons about mentoring another family who wanted to build true community in their neighborhood. The Johnsons felt honored to do so, and they took this family into their Home Group for three months to train them. At the end of this period of time, they prayed over them and released them to begin a Home Group and to establish a distinctly Christian presence in their own neighborhood. Although the dynamics were different, the results were similar. Soon they reproduced two additional groups and began a midsize gathering as well.

As the Johnsons were lying in bed one night, they marveled at how God was using them as his willing vessels beyond their wildest dreams. The sense of being a part of something so much greater than oneself overwhelmed the Johnsons, and they were filled with gratitude to God.

Volunteerism

During the time Bob and Karen were working on getting their busy schedules under control, they had pulled back from centralized church commitments. As they settled in to life in genuine community, they realized that the church as a whole needed them to participate in the Sunday and weekday ministry opportunities the Home Group didn't cover. Consequently, a major value for everyone in the Home Group was to do something to contribute to the broader ministry of their church. Some members served as ushers at worship services; others served in children and youth ministry. Still others served on the hospitality team. One member offered the services of his printing company, which would take the church's publications to the next level of excellence and impact. This attitude of volunteerism made for a wonderful marriage between the Home Group and the centralized church. Bob and Karen have come to see that this value of serving the church is an essential function of the neighborhood Home Group ministry; their pastor discovered that it is easier to recruit groups of people who are together in community than to recruit one person at a time.

International Missions

Because Bob had served on the church's missions committee, he knew that the church in America had a mission to fulfill in seeing the Christianity established in other parts of the world, particularly in those areas where there were unreached people groups. Bob and Karen's church was supporting a national pastor in Indonesia—the fourth-largest country in the world, with over 80 percent of its population being Muslim. The three Home Groups in the Johnsons' neighborhood agreed to adopt the native pastor, his family, and his vision as their own.

They did a number of practical things to connect to this significant work of supporting the planting of a church in Indonesia. First, they agreed to pray for them in intelligible ways. By connecting with the Indonesian pastor's supporting agency, they were able to stay informed about what was happening in this ministry. Second, all three Home Groups got together for an "Indonesian evening." They ate Indonesian food and told the children about the challenges of spreading the gospel in a Muslim-dominated country. The children were astonished to hear that Christians were persecuted for sharing their faith in Christ. Third, two of the Home Group families decided to use their vacation money to visit Indonesia. They took video cameras and linked up with a Western missionary who had grown up in Indonesia and who served as their host and translator. When the families returned, they showed the video and told incredible stories of the faith and the sacrifice they saw in that country. They are currently working on a strategy to develop an online connection between the kids they met in Indonesia and the kids in their families. While they are willing to provide the computers, the differences in language remains a barrier. Yet, with all the talents possessed by the members of the three Home Groups, they are sure to figure it out soon.

Bob and Karen feel strongly that they are not only being obedient to the Great Commission but that they are also giving their children the biblical view of Christian responsibility to the world.

Care

Caring for each other was one of the seven functions of the Home Group's covenant, but it wasn't something that could be scheduled. Their motto of care comes from the writings of King Solomon: "If one falls down, his friend can help him up. But pity the man who falls and has no one to help him up!"[2]

Over the course of the two years the Johnsons' Home Group had been together, three major events took place that called for the members to deploy their financial and human resources. The first was the death of Bob's mother after a long struggle with cancer. Throughout the whole ordeal, the church as a whole was sympathetic, but it was the Home Group members who got "up close and personal" through their expressions of care and compassion. Bob's mom lived in another part of the country; during the numerous times he had gone to visit her, the group members pitched in and helped Karen. They sent cards and wrote kind letters to Bob's family members. Together they pooled their money and bought a beautiful blanket for Bob's mom to use during her stay in the hospital. After Bob's mom passed away, several group members turned over their own frequent-flyer miles so the entire family could fly to the funeral without digging deep into their savings account. Bob and Karen commented often about how much more difficult this journey would have been without a genuine Christian community to support them.

The second event centered around a job loss experienced by a father in one of the Home Group families. The members of all three neighborhood Home Groups worked together to help the family during this transition. For two months they made sacrifices in order to help the family make their mortgage payment and pay their utility bills. Because this particular family had been so dedicated in helping Bob's family through their difficult time, the Johnsons were compelled to respond to this need. They were quick to take the step of reaching out in Christian love. The words of the apostle Paul kept echoing in Bob's head: "At the present time your plenty will supply what they need, so that in turn their plenty will supply what you need."[3]

The third major event to impact the Home Group families was the most difficult. One of the couples had been experiencing marital problems before they joined the

Home Group. Although this marriage had benefited from the relationships within the group for a time, the root of the problem had never been addressed. It became obvious to everyone that the relationship was becoming increasingly strained. When the family missed Home Group for two consecutive Sundays, using what seemed to be very weak excuses, the men in the group felt they had to respond. One morning they took the husband out to breakfast and confronted him lovingly about the man's marriage. In all honesty he told them that he and his wife just couldn't get along anymore and that he had no hope for reconciliation. At the core of the problem was the man's addiction to pornography on the Internet. The men committed to walk with him each step along the way toward release from his bondage—as long as he would make a commitment to stick with it. They also concluded that because any of them could stumble, they needed to hold each other accountable. So they agreed to have breakfast together once a month and ask each other a series of seven questions:

1. Devotions: Have you been spending time praying and reading Scripture each week?
2. Worship: Have you been taking your family to church each week?
3. Vocation: Have you been consistently putting in an honest week of work for your employer and for God?
4. Stewardship: Have you been staying above reproach in all your financial dealings?

5. Fidelity: Have you found yourself with a woman in the past weeks in such a way that would be inappropriate or could be viewed by others as a demonstration of poor judgment on your part?
6. Purity: Have you exposed yourself to any illicit material over the past weeks?
7. Priorities: Have you been spending sufficient time with your family each week?

It would have been tempting for the men to formulate lies in answer to these questions—and life would go on. However, because they were Christians, this community of men had been exposed to the light: "But if we walk in the light, as he is in the light, we have fellowship with one another, and the blood of Jesus, his Son, purifies us from all sin."[4] If one of them continued to walk in destructive darkness, he would not want to continue participating in the light; absence, therefore, would be the number one warning sign. What's more, because they lived in the same neighborhood, saw each other three to five times a week, and knew every member of the family, it would be difficult to lie. Living in holistic, authentic community has a way of keeping one honest.

There is good news with regard to this third difficult event. In the end, this marriage was strengthened. Although it has taken a significant amount of time to rebuild the trust, the process of restoration is well on its way.

This function of caring for each other is of paramount importance to the life of a church and the building of true community. Let me illustrate with a story. Recently Bob and

Karen saw a couple from their church in a store. The couple shared how their son had been in a car accident and had been in the hospital for three days. They lamented that while one of the pastors had stopped in for a visit, no one from the church really took a deep interest in them. They were thinking about leaving this church for a more caring one. Because the Johnsons were saddened by the thought of this family having had to go through this difficult experience alone, they expressed their sorrow to the mother and father and asked them if they had become involved in a Home Group, or something similar to it. The couple admitted that their involvement at church was pretty much limited to Sunday morning worship. This is exactly where Bob and Karen had been just two years ago, and they knew they would have reacted the same way if they had experienced what this couple experienced. Bob and Karen gently encouraged them to stay with the church and look into finding an existing Home Group to be involved in, or perhaps begin a Home Group in their own neighborhood.

Because this couple had been influenced by the culture of individualism, isolation, and consumerism, they responded unenthusiastically. To the Johnsons it looked as though they simply wanted to have their needs met without making the commitment to Christian community. The Johnsons understood this mind-set well and decided not to push. As the Johnsons left the store to go home, their spirit was not one of judgment but of pity for what this family was missing. How many churches would they need to move to until it dawned on them what the real problem was?

Extending Compassion

The final function the group gave themselves to was extending compassion in their community. The words of Jesus served as their inspiration:

> Then the King will say to those on his right, "Come, you who are blessed by my Father; take your inheritance, the kingdom prepared for you since the creation of the world. For I was hungry and you gave me something to eat, I was thirsty and you gave me something to drink, I was a stranger and you invited me in, I needed clothes and you clothed me, I was sick and you looked after me, I was in prison and you came to visit me."
>
> Then the righteous will answer him, 'Lord, when did we see you hungry and feed you, or thirsty and give you something to drink? When did we see you a stranger and invite you in, or needing clothes and clothe you? When did we see you sick or in prison and go to visit you?
>
> The King will reply, "I tell you the truth, whatever you did for one of the least of these brothers of mine, you did for me."[5]

For years the Johnsons had wanted to reach out to the bruised, the broken, and the abandoned strangers in the community. However, there had been so little time to give and no discretionary money available to use. But now they, along with other members of the body of Christ, were committed to extending compassion. Rather than go at it alone, they would combine their gifts to produce a greater and more effective return on their work.[6] They were also motivated to carry out this function because of their children. They reasoned that if their children were to participate in reaching out to the poor and needy, it would give them a more realistic perspective of the world around them. Perhaps it would prevent them from wasting precious time on the self-centered pursuit of consumerism; perhaps the call to be compassionate would be so ingrained in their children by the time they left the nest that it would be considered the only appropriate way of life. Perhaps their children would not have to wait until they were thirty or forty years old to truly understand the words of Paul: "In everything I did, I showed you that by this kind of hard work we must help the weak, remembering the words the Lord Jesus himself said: 'It is more blessed to give than to receive.'"[7]

The Home Group families met together to discuss practical steps they could take to extend compassion to the weak and the suffering. They wanted both to make a long-term commitment that had some continuity to it and to be available to help in the community on a onetime basis. After much prayer and reflection, the group decided to work with an independent agency in the community to adopt a homeless family and help them get on their feet financially, socially, and spiritually. This family had been approved to be a part of a two-year program, which would not be funded by the government. The husband, who had a wife and three beautiful children, had been incarcerated for writing bad checks. The sponsoring agency owned a home where this family was to live; in return the family would pay an amount in keeping with their income. The agency provided a caseworker and job training for the father following his release from prison.

The Home Group had very practical, as well as relational and spiritual, purposes in their involvement with this family. They would help repair the house, have them as part of their Home Group once a month, celebrate their children's birthdays, give advice and counsel, and, most important, show them they were deeply loved by a group of human beings who have been touched by the love of Jesus Christ. While there were learning experiences along the way and a few bumps in the road, the family graduated from the program six months earlier than planned. The husband became a Christian; the wife was already a Christian, but she renewed her faith commitment. The family ended up joining a church in another part of town. Today the father is a board member of the agency that helped him get back on his feet. The Home Group concluded that all the challenges were worth it in the end; what they had done together was a very important aspect of fulfilling the will of God.

There were times in their experience of authentic community when the Johnsons were tired; they would have preferred to stay home and watch television when Sunday night rolled around. Yet they recognized that living in Christian community is not all about comfort and convenience; it is all about hard work and sometimes sacrificial giving in order to fulfill the requirements of Christ's command to love one another. Community is about giving yourself entirely to Christ and to your neighbor. In turn and in time, the investment comes back to you tenfold. The Johnsons concluded that the Christian life takes commitment, by all means, but in the end the yoke of Jesus is easy.[8]

As they spent more and more time with the other families in their neighborhood, the Johnsons noticed idiosyncrasies about the families that irritated them, but they wisely understood that this is the way family life goes. There were things Bob did that annoyed Karen, and things Karen did that annoyed Bob. Whenever you spend enough time together to achieve a degree of intimacy, you must live with the quirks that come with those relationships. If you are going to truly live life together in Christian community, you are not going to be able to hold up the "I'm perfect" front forever. Once we get past our desire to impress other people, we can move toward having a real impact in each other's lives. Accepting each other just the way we are is a necessary and wonderful part of true Christian community.

After the first two years of their experience of neighborhood Home Group community life, the Johnsons vowed that they would never go back to the individualistic, isolated lifestyle of consumerism that had governed their lives for more than thirty years. They also recognized that they had a long way to go in their quest to learn more about Christ and to become more like him; the mysteries of authentic Christian community would take a lifetime to learn.[9] The Johnsons signed up for the duration.

14

IMPLEMENTING COMMON

POSSESSIONS

_____

_____

_____

A few years ago our church sponsored a couple from London, England, to serve an internship with our church's student ministries and to attend seminary. Their life in London was similar to ours—filled with automobiles and material things and overbooked schedules. When they came to America, they left all that behind. Our church put them up in a home we owned, which happened to be in our neighborhood. One day I was talking with the husband and realized that they didn't have an automobile to drive. His wife worked at the Christian school operated by our church and located within walking distance of their house; the husband needed to travel to Dallas to attend classes three days a week. I could easily walk to work, and often did, so I offered to let him borrow my car to attend his seminary classes. He took me up on my offer.

Here's how it worked: Three days a week Rob came to our house in the morning and picked up my car. He

attended school all day; in the evening, around 9:00 or
10:00 P.M., he pulled into our back driveway. As he drove
in he would see my wife and me sitting in the family room.
Each night he returned the keys and always stayed for a
short visit. After a week, I noticed that his wife, Keren,
would be in the car with him. (Before he returned the car,
he would stop by his house and pick up his wife.) Now, we
had the opportunity to enjoy their company three nights a
week. This transaction alone gave us six relational encounters a week.

This went on for about a year when one day they came
over to our house on one of those Texas one-hundred-
degree-plus summer days. We were in the backyard with
about twenty other people who were there to help us celebrate the birthday of one of our children. Rob and Keren
asked if they could borrow the large air blower from the
church. Out of curiosity I asked why, and they explained
that their air conditioner had stopped working. Without
blinking an eye, I invited them to stay with us until their
unit was fixed. They agreed, and for the next seven days we
enjoyed the company of this lovely couple. While I struggle to spend personal time with the members of our
church's large staff, here I was spending every day with one
of our interns—and enjoying every minute of it.

One day Rob came into my office with a poignant
observation about community: What made our relationship
so special, he said, was not just living in the same neighborhood but the fact that *they needed us.* That day I learned
the power of interdependence as an essential principle of
authentic community. Now that I'm looking everywhere
for signs of its presence, I can see how it significantly helped

bond the community of the first-century church. Passages like Acts 4:32–37 and 2 Corinthians 8:1–15 give us insight into the beauty of interdependent relationships. I would suggest that one of the major obstacles to community in America is that we don't need each other anymore. We are *independent* people. As a matter of fact, nearly all expression of American charity has as its goal to make people independent, just like we are. Sadly, when a person becomes independent of others, they get the loneliness and isolation that accompany it as well.

By the way, three things happened to dismantle our wonderful arrangement of community with our friends from London: The air conditioning was repaired, my wife and I gave the couple a car, and we moved to a different neighborhood. While we still love and enjoy Rob and Keren immensely, our relationship is no longer spontaneous or frequent; no longer are we dependent on each other.

One of the most wonderful sights in the entire world is to witness a small band of people living together in a neighborhood and being the body of Christ. We have learned that authentic community is not just a meeting together, but a *way of life* together. Affinity groups may produce a "meeting time" that is as good, or even better, than a Christian neighborhood community, but it can't come close to producing the wonderful life experienced *between* the meetings!

INTRODUCING THE VALUES OF COMMON POSSESSIONS

How do the leaders in a local church go about introducing the values of *common possessions* into a *common place* so that a *common purpose* is accomplished? We value decentralized ministry, that is to say, we are committed to doing ministry in and through our Community Group and Home Group structure. Setting ourselves up in this way promotes the highest level of ownership and empowerment and thus produces the greatest amount of fruit at the end of the day. Below are three principles that undergird decentralization while at the same time defining the role of the central leadership of the church.

Decentralized but Purpose Driven

The leaders of the church have defined the broad vision and parameters for the common purpose of true community. While each group expresses these purposes in different and creative ways, we are all pursuing the same thing. For our particular vision, we want all groups to be geographically based, to use the Christian Life Profile as a common creed, and to pursue the Seven Functions of Biblical Community as the primary purpose of the corporate gathering.

Decentralized but Supported

While each gathering is empowered to make and carry out decisions on how they will approach the common purpose, our church does provide central support. The zone pastor is the primary overseer of training and assistance. In addition, we have formed teams that help make the work of the Home Group more effective and efficient. For example, we have a Compassion Team that represents different agencies in our community. Their job is to alert our Home Groups to the needs of each agency. In a sense they become brokers of compassion ministry. As a Home Group you would look at these opportunities and then pray and discuss among yourselves the direction you will take in extending compassion to the needy in your local community.

Decentralized but Centralized Praise

To promote authentic community the central pastoral leadership highlights success stories in gatherings like the worship service and through media such as newsletters and a Web page. We have created video testimonies of Community Groups or Home Groups who care for each other, lead people in their neighborhood to Christ, reach out in compassion to the needy, or go "over the top" in doing something to support the work of the church internationally. These promotional pieces encourage the people who are engaged in community life and inspire those who are not yet involved in community life to give it a try.

IMPLEMENTING THE FUNCTIONS OF COMMUNITY

In chapter 12 I presented five characteristics of authentic community that promote common possessions—interdependency, intergenerational life, children, responsibility, and sacrifice. Because our church believes these characteristics must be present if genuine community is to exist, we have made several significant decisions about the structure of Home Groups—interdependency should be promoted, including giving authority and responsibility to Home Group members to do the work of ministry; the gatherings should be intergenerational; and children should be involved.

Interdependency Promoted

The leadership of the church is constantly promoting interdependency. We attempt to teach this and lead it by example. Essentially we invite our people to lean on each other in our mutual quest to meet needs both inside and outside the group. We are asking them to pool their financial resources, material possessions, and spiritual gifts in order to accomplish the purposes of the church. The average Bible study small group draws predominantly on the gifts of teaching; the neighborhood Home Group draws on every gift of every person in order to fulfill its purpose—from hospitality and mercy to leadership and evangelism. If they don't combine these resources, the community will fail in accomplishing its overall mission and its specific tasks.

SPIRITUAL FORMATION

Home Group members are invited to use the Christian Life Profile assessment tool and then to share the results with each other. Every member of the group selects at least one to three areas of the Christian Life Profile to work on throughout the year. Everyone agrees to interdependently support and pray for each other in their individual spiritual quest. There is no ordained pastor to lead the people through the process; there is no priest to whom people confess their sins—members of the Home Group do this for each other as the "royal priesthood" of believers.[1]

EVANGELISM

We have made the task of evangelism a high priority for our Home Groups. We call it *community evangelism*, and it is as effective as any method I've seen. Members of the Home Group pray for and connect with those in their area who are unchurched or non-Christians—as well as with Christians in their neighborhood who attend other churches.

In the natural flow of everyday life, a member of a Home Group will often invite one other family in the Home Group and a new neighbor over for a barbecue or invite them to go out for dinner. In our neighborhood the men of the Home Group get together to play basketball every Wednesday evening. This is a great opportunity to invite other men to join us and to get to know each other. When the time is right, the Home Group member will usually invite these men either to a worship service or to a Community Group or Home Group gathering. Zone pastors train Home Group leaders in how to be intentional about evangelism. We know that if non-Christians can see true Christian community—bathed in love and compassion—being lived out in a neighborhood, they will be drawn to the God whose grace and power undergirds it all.

REPRODUCTION

Home Groups and Community Groups take the responsibility to launch new groups from their nucleus as they grow in numbers. We encourage them to launch a new group in twelve- to twenty-four-month cycles. As the groups launch, a greater geographic density is created.

VOLUNTEERISM

We have asked members of Community Groups and Home Groups to fill the volunteer positions necessary to carry out our ministry on Sunday mornings as we gather centrally (worship involvement, ushering, hospitality ministry, and the like) and to be a part of the youth and children ministries, assisting the children and youth in their spiritual development. Without question, the highest percentage of volunteers comes from the people who are part of our Community Groups and Home Groups. Time and time again we see these folks take up the slack in helping to carry out the mission of the church centrally.

International Missions

We do not have a missions committee at our church to dispense funds for international church projects; rather, we delegate this task to the Community Groups and Home Groups. The elders have set out a broad vision for where they believe we need to focus our energy, and then they set a budget. The funds are distributed to the zone pastors, who in turn go to the Home Group members to ask them to prayerfully decide where the money is to be spent. Home Group members contact the five approved agencies on our list and work with them on projects we could support over the course of a year. Our involvement might include purchasing equipment or contributing to the salary or training of a national pastor.

Once the decision on the type of involvement is made, Home Groups are responsible to stay connected to the ongoing details of the project. Members are free to get involved in any way they would like. Some have given up their family vacation for the year as they travel to the location to observe the work and to offer their assistance. Ownership of missions goals soars when people have a vested interest and are given the responsibility to decide how to become involved. We are currently putting together a team to help facilitate the success of this process. They are not the decision makers but rather the facilitators who will assist the Home Groups in carrying out their common purpose.

CARE

Our care ministries have by and large been assigned to our Community Groups and Home Groups under the leadership of the zone pastor. If there is a need within the Home Group itself, this group is trained to meet the need. It could involve things like the benevolent giving of money to those in need or an intervention in the case of an addiction. If the need goes beyond the resources and gifts of the Home Group, the leader talks with the Community Group shepherd about the participation of the larger group in helping to meet the need. If the need goes beyond the resources or gifts of the Community Group, the Community Group shepherd goes to his zone pastor, who talks to other zone pastors as appropriate to enlist the help of the broader set of Community Groups. From time to time, a request comes from our zone pastors that requires the financial or spiritual assistance of the central eldership of the church. This may include the exercise of the biblical duty of church discipline. While the elders of the church are involved spiritually in the process of church discipline, the leaders of a particular geographic zone responsibly and sensitively takes the necessary biblical steps to fulfill their spiritual calling. It has been awesome to see how this works!

EXTENDING COMPASSION

Just as we have done for international missions, we have assigned our local compassion efforts to the Home Group. Members might choose to build a home for Habitat for Humanity or to serve once a month at the night shelter;

they might adopt a homeless family or work at the local pregnancy center's resale shop. It has been extraordinarily exciting to watch how this level of ownership is facilitating more outreach into the local community than a centralized "compassion office" could ever do. Ten years ago, our church was not making a substantial deposit of Christian love in our local community; today we are receiving awards from many local compassion organizations for being "the community of faith of the year." We believe this is because we are becoming a gathering of believers in a common place, interdependently working together to fulfill the common purpose Jesus Christ gave us to love our neighbor and to help the poor.

Intergenerational Groups

A second decision we implemented based on the characteristics of authentic community is to make the gatherings intergenerational. We believe this may be one of the most dynamic and important decisions we've made to this point. Seeing grandparents in a room with middle-aged parents, young adults, college students, singles, and children of all ages looks like a picture out of the photo albums of the "First Church of Jerusalem."

When we promote true community in our literature, in our worship services, or on our Web page, we simply encourage each person to visit the group located in their particular area. More and more people are finding intergenerational community to be an incredibly rich experience. While many today talk about the values of intergenerational living, the people of our church are doing it. I'm proud of the people in our church who have been able to break out of the strong grip of niche marketing and exclusive life-stage gatherings.

The Presence of Children

Children and youth are encouraged to attend Home Groups, for it is truly the place where the Christian life is lived out, the place where a band of people put their faith into action. The purpose of the Home Group is involvement in the Christian life. It would be a shame to deprive our children and young people of the experience of learning firsthand how Christian community works. No longer is the family segregated; now we have come together to do everything that Christ commanded. It is here that the Christian life is not *taught,* but *caught!*

What do the children do? In essence, they participate in the fulfillment of the Seven Functions of Biblical Community. As you review chapter 13, imagine the children being involved in each activity. The central leadership of our church provides the materials and assistance to make the task of the Home Group leader easier and more effective. We supply written object lessons that can be used in the Home Group to allow an opportunity for adults to instruct the children in the Christian Life Profile. Our worship pastor supplies worship songbooks that include songs for adults, children, and youth. The central leadership is always looking for ways to facilitate the positive presence of children in the group.

Is the presence of children always comfortable? By no means! They can do for the Home Group family what they often do for the nuclear family, namely, create chaos! But in the end, having the children present simply feels right. The children also create a highly motivational environment. Parents often walk home feeling deeply encouraged that they were together that night as a family in spiritual community. Usually at some point in the weekly gathering, a child says or does or sees something the adults know is contributing to the child's spiritual development. While not all of our groups have embraced the presence of children in their Home Groups, we unashamedly lift up this historical value and essential principle of authentic community.

AFTERWORD

The story of the Johnsons is my story—not literally, but in terms of the overall shared feelings of suburban individualism, isolation, and consumerism. Our family, too, had been running frantically in all directions but experiencing little depth in our connections with others—or with each other. *Community* was eluding my family and me, even though I served as pastor of a good-sized suburban church. The fact is, being the pastor of a large church of individuals may be among the loneliest and most frustrating jobs in the world. Frankly, there are days when I wonder if all the pain is worth it. Of this, though, I am convinced: The mission of the church cannot be accomplished apart from Christian community. If Christian community is not available or is not being pursued, what can we really hope to accomplish together as a church and as individuals who really do long to belong? I repeat the words of Bruderhof Communities founder Eberhard Arnold: "Efforts to organize community artificially can only result in ugly, lifeless caricatures."[1]

I began my journey of rediscovering the beauty of relationships, the concept of neighborhood, and the strength of interdependence a number of years ago. The preliminary results are contained in this book, disguised in the lives of Bob and Karen Johnson. I'm in the process of leading the church I pastor in this direction. To date, the results have been very meaningful. As of the writing of this book, we have five full-time zone pastors, twenty-seven geographically centered Community Groups, and sixty-eight Home Groups. Our vision for the next ten years is to have twenty full-time zone pastors, one hundred Community Groups, and over five hundred Home Groups, built on the principles of this book. That tallies over 12,000 people engaged in authentic biblical community. The dream that others might discover the wonder and joy of true Christian community—now that's what gets me out of bed in the morning to face another day.

I have a son who was born without a left hand. One day in Sunday school the teacher was talking with the children about the church. To illustrate her point she folded her hands together and said, "Here's the church, here's the steeple; open the doors and see all the people." She asked the class to do it along with her—obviously not thinking about my son's inability to pull this exercise off. Yet in the next moment it dawned on her that my son could not join in. Before she could do anything about it, the little boy next to my son, a friend of his from the time they were babies, reached out his left hand and said, "Let's do it together." The two boys proceeded to join their hands together to make the church and the steeple. This hand exercise should never be done again by an individual because the church is not a collection of individuals, but the one body of Christ.

I wrote *The Connecting Church* in order to share the principles I am learning about authentic biblical community, principles gleaned both from my study of the Bible and from my conversations with other people. These foundational principles are at this very moment alive and intact; bear in mind, though, that because the ideas presented here, while ancient, are so new and fresh to the church of the twenty-first century, you can rest assured that Pantego Bible Church will always be exploring new ways to improve on what we have begun.

I offer three solutions for stimulating effective community, solutions built on a set of fifteen characteristics. One set of five characteristics supports the premise that authentic community requires a *common purpose*, another collection reestablishes the ancient principle that true community involves the sharing of a *common place*, while the final five characteristics suggest strongly that if we are to recover any semblance of community in our relationships as Christians, we must come to realize that everything we are and everything we have as *common possessions* should be used to promote godly connections.

The central obstacle to the rediscovery of these principles is the reality that all of them are countercultural. All of them run against the grain of the reigning priorities of individualism, isolation, and consumerism. Herein lies the difficulty for church leaders who are responsible to promote the kind of transformational Christian community that powerfully represents the presence of Christ on earth. It is not easy to advance toward a common purpose, a common place, and common possessions all at once. Most leaders do not have enough "pocket change" of trust to pay the price for this kind of large-scale change.

Some of you who read these words will not be convinced of all three solutions. I anticipate a number of church leaders embracing the principles that drive a *common purpose* but not a *common place*. Navigating the rediscovery of neighborhood may be the toughest of all challenges. Some of you may not believe that espousing this principle is necessary in order to embrace genuine community. This is a perfectly legitimate belief. This journey to assess authentic Christian community is a learning experience for all of us, with a diversity of opinion on the best approach. Certainly, not everyone in our congregation sees the need for geography to be an organizing principle for community.

I firmly believe that the other two principles can aid in the discovery of community, even if you do not organize community around place (neighborhood). While my personal experience makes the benefits of this three-pronged view of community very real to me, I openly confess that this is not an all-or-nothing proposition. If you embrace certain principles proposed here, and not others, apply what you embrace with great conviction. In my estimation, the application of *any* of the characteristics of community will dynamically enhance the life of your congregation. Therefore, converse with the Lord on what to apply and when, and then proceed to do that—nothing more, nothing less.

My driving motivation is that all who read these words will be so intrigued, so attracted, that they will want to set out on this journey toward genuine community as well. I prayerfully hope you will carefully ponder what is humbly presented here—words ultimately offered to God for his use and for his glory—and, most important, that you will not just put the book down and go on with life as usual, but that you will make a firm decision about what you are going to do about what you have just read. True Christian community is available. Get connected!

I am confident that if you and your church venture out on this journey of authentic community, you too will add insights and discoveries we can all benefit from. As you begin taking steps to build a connecting church, you'll have exciting stories to tell along the way. I'd love to have you share them with me and with all whose hearts beat to see the church recapture the essence of Christian community. Contact us at:

response@TheConnectingChurch.com

APPENDIX

SPIRITUAL FORMATION CALENDAR

_____

_____

_____

SAMPLE FROM THE YEAR 2000

Date	Model Emphasis	Date	Model Emphasis
Core Beliefs: First Five		_Core Practices: First Five_	
Jan. 2	Trinity	Mar. 26	Prayer
Jan. 9	Trinity	Apr. 2	Prayer
Jan. 16	Trinity	Apr. 9	Worship
Jan. 23	Salvation by Grace	Apr. 16	Worship (Palm Sunday)
Jan. 30	Salvation by Grace	Apr. 23	Open Sunday (Easter)
Feb. 6	Authority of the Bible	Apr. 30	Single-Mindedness
Feb. 13	Authority of the Bible	May 7	Single-Mindedness
Feb. 20	Personal God	May 14	Bible Study
Feb. 27	Personal God	May 21	Bible Study
Mar. 5	Identity in Christ	May 28	Giving Away Our Life
Mar. 12	Identity in Christ		
Mar. 19	Identity in Christ		

Date	Model Emphasis	Date	Model Emphasis
Core Virtues: First Five		*Core Practices: Second Five*	
June 4	Joy	Sept. 17	Biblical Community
June 11	Peace	Sept. 24	Biblical Community
June 18	Hope	Oct. 1	Spiritual Gifts
June 25	Faith(fulness)	Oct. 8	Giving Away Our Faith
July 2	Self-Control	Oct. 15	Giving Away Our Time
		Oct. 22	Giving Away Our Money
Core Beliefs: Second Five			
July 9	Church	*Core Virtues: Second Five*	
July 16	Church		
July 23	Humanity	Oct. 29	Love
July 30	Humanity	Nov. 5	Humility
Aug. 6	Compassion	Nov. 12	Patience
Aug. 13	Compassion	Nov. 19	Kindness/Goodness
Aug. 20	Eternity	Nov. 26	Gentleness
Aug. 27	Eternity		
Sept. 3	Stewardship	*Advent Season*	
Sept. 10	Stewardship		
		Dec. 3	Prophecy
		Dec. 10	Bethlehem
		Dec. 17	Shepherds
		Dec. 24	Angels
		Dec. 31	Open Sunday

NOTES

PREFACE: OPENING WORDS

1. Within each of the three parts of this book I will cover five characteristics that must be present in order for genuine community to be experienced.

CHAPTER 1: THE LONELIEST NATION ON EARTH

1. Noted in his book, *The People's Religion* (New York: Macmillan, 1989).
2. Noted in Philip Langdon, *A Better Place to Live: Reshaping the American Suburb* (New York: HarperPerennial, 1994), 1.

CHAPTER 2: CREATED FOR COMMUNITY

1. Cited in Joe G. Emerson, *I Wanted the Elevator, but I Got the Shaft: Inspiration for Life's Ups & Downs* (Nashville: Dimensions for Living, 1993), 37.
2. George Gallup Jr., *Emerging Trends,* vol. 19, no. 3 (March 1997).
3. Hebrews 10:25, emphasis added.
4. Matthew 16:18.
5. Wayne A. Meeks, *The First Urban Christians: The Social World of the Apostle Paul* (New Haven, Conn.: Yale Univ. Press, 1984), 78.
6. From a speech given by Lyle Schaller at a Leadership Network Conference in Ontario, California, October 1998.

CHAPTER 3: THE PROBLEM OF INDIVIDUALISM

1. Transcribed from *Antz,* Eric Darnell and Tim Johnson, directors; Todd Alcott, Chris Weitz, and Paul Weitz, screenplay (Dreamworks, 1998).
2. See Philippians 3:7–11.
3. See Philippians 2:3–4.
4. See E. D. Hirsch Jr., *Cultural Literacy* (Boston: Houghton Mifflin, 1987).

5. John L. Locke, *The De-Voicing of Society: Why We Don't Talk to Each Other Anymore* (New York: Simon & Schuster, 1998), 122. The time immediately following World War II represented a prosperous era for the American economy. The resources paid for the advancement of the superhighway system, which, under Dwight Eisenhower's presidency, made mobility possible and diminished rooted relationships. This boom time also sparked the rise of suburban living, where close-knit neighborhoods were forfeited in favor of individual privacy. In addition, technological developments, such as central air and heating, refrigeration, and the television, have prompted many suburbanites to stay cocooned in their homes for the few hours they are actually there each day. The reality of easy mobility has resulted in Americans spending much of their time in the automobile and not in the home. I'll have more to say about this in part 2.

6. Quoted in Locke, *The De-Voicing of Society*, 125.

7. See Hirsch, *Cultural Literacy*, xvii.

8. See Genesis 2:18.

9. Locke, *The De-Voicing of Society*, 202–203.

10. See Robert Wuthnow, *Sharing the Journey: Support Groups and America's New Quest for Community* (New York: Free Press, 1994).

11. 2 Peter 1:3–11.

12. George Barna, *The Barna Update* (12 July 2000), biweekly e-mail report from George Barna.

13. Dallas Willard, *The Spirit of the Disciplines* (New York: HarperCollins, 1988), 16.

14. Personal conversation with Dallas Willard (4 October 1999).

15. John 1:17.

16. Romans 3:23.

17. See John 4:1–42.

18. See John 8:1–11.

19. Ephesians 4:15.

20. Ephesians 4:16.

Chapter 4: Finding a Common Purpose

1. Wayne A. Meeks, *The First Urban Christians: The Social World of the Apostle Paul* (New Haven, Conn.: Yale Univ. Press, 1983), 75.

2. John L. Locke, *The De-Voicing of Society: Why We Don't Talk to Each Other Anymore* (New York: Simon & Schuster, 1998), 131.

3. Meeks, *The First Urban Christians*, 76.

4. Meeks, *The First Urban Christians*, 93. An *argot* is a private vocabulary used within a community as a way to summarize entire paragraphs of meaning by means of a single word or collection of words.

5. Deuteronomy 6:20–25.

6. See 1 Corinthians 11:26.

7. Acts 2:44.

8. Acts 2:42.

9. Acts 4:32.

10. Ephesians 4:4–6.

11. Lyle Schaller, "Every Part Is an 'I': How Will the Body Function in an Age of Rising Individualism," *Leadership Journal* (Fall 1999), 29.

12. Cited in George Gallup Jr., *Emerging Trends,* vol. 19, no. 2 (February 1997), quoted in a speech given by Gallup at the annual luncheon of the Laymen's National Bible Association on November 22, 1996.

13. Schaller, "Every Part Is an 'I,'" 29.

14. C. S. Lewis, *Mere Christianity* (New York: Macmillan, 1943), 163, 169–70.

15. Galatians 4:19; also see Ephesians 4:15–16; Colossians 1:28–29

16. Dallas Willard, *The Spirit of the Disciplines* (New York: HarperCollins, 1988), 16.

17. See Romans 12:1–2; Philippians 4:8.

18. See Philippians 4:9; 1 Timothy 4:8; Hebrews 5:13–14.

19. See Philippians 2:5.

20. Philippians 2:1–5.

21. See 2 Peter 1:3–11.

22. Willard, *The Spirit of the Disciplines,* 16.

CHAPTER 5: REDISCOVERING BIBLICAL PURPOSE

1. Dallas Willard, *The Spirit of the Disciplines* (New York: HarperCollins, 1988), 16.

2. Luke 10:27.

3. John 15:9–12.

4. See also 1 John 4:10, 19.

5. George Gallup Jr., *Emerging Trends,* vol. 19, no. 2 (February 1997), 1.

6. George Barna, *The Habits of Highly Effective Churches* (Ventura, Calif.: Regal, 2000), 10.

7. Dieter and Valerie Zander, "The Evolution of Gen X Ministry," *re:generation quarterly,* vol. 5, no. 3 (Fall 1999), 19.

8. See Romans 12:1–2.

9. See Psalms 19 and 119; Hebrews 5:7.

10. 2 Peter 3:18.

11. There is probably no greater collection than the one commonly known as the "fruit of the Spirit," recorded in Galatians 5:22–23. According to psychiatrist David Larson, "It would be difficult to concoct a better recipe for health"—cited in Philip Yancey, "Finding God in Unexpected Places," *The Christian Reader* (July/August 1995), 10.

12. See George Gallup Jr. and Timothy Jones, *The Saints Among Us* (Harrisburg, Pa.: Morehouse, 1992), 10.

13. See Romans 12:1–8.

14. See Ephesians 4:16.

15. See John 13:35.

16. Gleaned from Larry Crabb and Dwight Edwards, "The Power of Connecting" conference, Dallas, Texas, October 1998.

17. Eberhard Arnold, *Why We Live in Community* (Farmington, Pa.: Plough Publishing House, 1995), 21.

CHAPTER 6: IMPLEMENTING A COMMON PURPOSE

1. Bob Buford, *Halftime* (Grand Rapids: Zondervan, 1997).

2. See Luke 10:27.

3. See Hebrews 4:12.

CHAPTER 7: THE PROBLEM OF ISOLATION

1. *Boston Globe* story, "Years After Neighbors Last Saw Her, Worcester Woman Found Dead in Home," quoted in Jacqueline Olds, Richard Schwartz, and Harriet Webster, *Overcoming Loneliness in Everyday Life* (Secaucus, N.J.: Carol Publishing Group, 1996), 28–29.

2. Liz Stevens, "Suburbia: Are Suburbs Hazardous to Your Health?" *Fort Worth Star-Telegram* (8 March 1997), 6.

3. Quoted in Stevens, "Suburbia," 6.

4. See Stevens, "Suburbia," 6.

5. Philip Langdon, *A Better Place to Live: Reshaping the American Suburb* (New York: HarperPerennial, 1994), 1.

6. James Howard Kunstler, "Home from Nowhere," *Atlantic Monthly* (September 1996), 43.

7. John L. Locke, *The De-Voicing of Society: Why We Don't Talk to Each Other Anymore* (New York: Simon & Schuster, 1998), 118–22.

8. Locke, *The De-Voicing of Society,* 122.

CHAPTER 8: FINDING A COMMON PLACE

1. Transcribed from *Jurassic Park*, Steven Spielberg, director; Michael Crichton and David Koepp, screenplay (based on the book by Michael Crichton), Universal City Studios and Amblin Entertainment, 1993.

2. Jeremiah 6:16.

3. *Merriam-Webster's Intermediate Dictionary*, s.v. "spontaneity."

4. John L. Locke, *The De-Voicing of Society: Why We Don't Talk to Each Other Anymore* (New York: Simon & Schuster, 1998), 122.

5. Noted in "The People Have Spoken," *Fort Worth Star-Telegram* (8 December 1996), sec. A, p. 24.

6. See Luke 10:25–37.

7. Quoted in Edward J. Blakely and Mary Gail Snyder, *Fortress America: Gated Communities in the United States* (Washington, D.C.: Brookings Institution Press, 1997), 35.

8. Acts 2:42.

9. Acts 2:46.

10. Locke, *The De-Voicing of Society,* 132.

11. Jim Petersen, *Discipleship Journal,* vol. 12, no. 3, issue 69 (May/June 1992), 92.

12. Jeffrey Weiss, "Your church is largely what it eats, author says," *Dallas Morning News* (24 July 1999), Religion section.

13. Acts 2:46.

14. Eberhard Arnold, *Why We Live in Community* (Farmington, Pa.: Plough Publishing House, 1995), 17.

15. Henri Nouwen, *The Inner Voice of Love: A Journey Through Anguish to Freedom* (New York: Doubleday, 1996), xiii–xiv.

16. Larry Crabb, *Connecting: A Radical New Vision* (Nashville: Word, 1997), 23–24.

17. Jenell Williams Paris, "Why I no longer live in community," *re:generation quarterly,* vol. 5, no. 2 (Summer 1999), 10.

CHAPTER 9: REDISCOVERING NEIGHBORHOOD

1. Robert Wuthnow, *Sharing the Journey: Support Groups and America's New Quest for Community* (New York: Free Press, 1994), 276.

2. Wuthnow, *Sharing the Journey,* 276–77.

3. Eric Pooley, "The Great Escape: Americans are fleeing suburbia for small towns. Do their lives equal their dreams?" *Time* (8 December 1997), 54.

4. See Acts 2:47

5. Matthew 7:12

6. It should be noted that some groups of Christians set aside Saturday as their day of worship and spiritual focus.

7. Wayne A. Meeks, *The First Urban Christians: The Social World of the Apostle Paul* (New Haven, Conn.: Yale Univ. Press, 1983), 105.

8. Lyle Schaller, *Discontinuity and Hope: A Radical Change and the Path to the Future* (Nashville: Abingdon, 1999), 11.

CHAPTER 10: IMPLEMENTING A COMMON PLACE

1. David Wells, "The Price of Modern Rootlessness," quoted by Ken Myers on Mars Hill Audio, "Anthologies, Number 3: Place, Community, and Memory" (Powhaten, Va.: Berea Publications Inc., 2000).

2. William Leach, *Country of Exiles: The Destruction of Place in American Life* (New York: Pantheon, 1999), quoted by Ken Myers on Mars Hill Audio, "Anthologies, Number 3: Place, Community, and Memory" (Powhaten, Va.: Berea Publications Inc., 2000).

3. Cited in Liz Stevens, "Party of One," *Fort Worth Star-Telegram* (30 July 2000), Life section, p. G1.

4. Robert Putnam, a "Surprising Fact" noted on the Internet Web site www.bowlingalone.com.

5. Lyle Schaller, *Discontinuity and Hope: A Radical Change and the Path to the Future* (Nashville: Abingdon, 1999), 57.

6. Schaller, *Discontinuity and Hope,* 57.

7. Schaller, *Discontinuity and Hope,* 60.

8. Schaller, *Discontinuity and Hope,* 60.

9. Everett M. Rogers, *Diffusion of Innovations,* 4th ed. (New York: Free Press, 1995), 262.

10. Robert Putnam, *Bowling Alone: The Collapse and Revival of American Community* (New York: Simon & Schuster, 2000), 391.

11. Putnam, *Bowling Alone,* 391.

CHAPTER 11: THE PROBLEM OF CONSUMERISM

1. Matthew 7:12.

2. See Matthew 6:24.

3. John L. Locke, *The De Voicing of Society: Why We Don't Talk to Each Other Anymore* (New York: Simon & Schuster, 1998), 156.

4. Quoted in Locke, *The De-Voicing of Society,* 156.

5. George Gallup Jr. and Timothy Jones, *The Saints Among Us* (Harrisburg, Pa.: Morehouse, 1992), 10.

6. See Matthew 5:39–41.

7. 1 Corinthians 6:1–8.

8. Locke, *The De-Voicing of Society,* 154.

9. See Exodus 20:17; Colossians 3:5

10. Philip Langdon, *A Better Place to Live: Reshaping the American Suburb* (New York: HarperPerennial, 1994), 240.

11. See Philippians 4:13.

CHAPTER 12: SHARING COMMON POSSESSIONS

1. Acts 4:32–37.

2. Acts 5:1–2.

3. Acts 4:32b.

4. Quoted by Martin Marty in *Context.*

5. Matthew 4:4.

6. See John 6:35.

7. 2 Corinthians 8:13–15.

8. See 1 Samuel 15:22.

9. Psalm 37:4.

10. Luke 12:48b.

11. Quoted in John L. Locke, *The De Voicing of Society: Why We Don't Talk to Each Other Anymore* (New York: Simon & Schuster, 1998), 137.

12. See Titus 2:1-15.

13. Noted by George Gallup Jr., "The Healing of America," *Emerging Trends,* vol. 19, no. 3 (March 1997), 4.

14. Quoted in Dieter and Valerie Zander, "The Evolution of Gen X Ministry," *re:generation quarterly,* vol. 5, no. 3 (Fall 1999), 19.

15. Zander, "The Evolution of Gen X Ministry," 17.

16. Quoted in Locke, *The DeVoicing of Society,* 137.

17. Philippians 2:1–5.

18. 1 John 3:16–20.

19. Eberhard Arnold, *Why We Live in Community* (Farmington, Pa.: Plough Publishing House, 1995), 18.

20. Matthew 16:24–25.

21. Noted in Edward J. Blakely and Mary Gail Snyder, *Fortress America: Gated Communities in the United States* (Washington, D.C.: Brookings Institution Press, 1997), 31.

22. Arnold, *Why We Live in Community,* 13.

CHAPTER 13: REDISCOVERING INTERDEPENDENCE

1. See James 5:16.

2. Ecclesiastes 4:10.

3. 2 Corinthians 8:14.

4. 1 John 1:7.

5. Matthew 25:34–40.

6. See Ecclesiastes 4:9.

7. Acts 20:35.

8. See Matthew 11:29-30.

9. See Ephesians 4:32.

CHAPTER 14: IMPLEMENTING COMMON POSSESSIONS

1. 1 Peter 2:9.

AFTERWORD

1. Eberhard Arnold, *Why We Live in Community* (Farmington, Pa.: Plough Publishing House, 1995), 13.